A View from the Pews

The Inside Story of a Broken Church

D1369547

For the victims —

JST
2023

Joy S. Taylor

Lily of the Valley Publishing, Inc.
Santa Claus, Indiana 47579 USA | 812.661.1323 |
www.mylilyofthevalley.org |
publishing@mylilyofthevalley.org

Dedication

I dedicate this work to the victims of abuse, whether physical, emotional, sexual, or spiritual. I also dedicate this work to those who have boldly spoken out and confronted their abusers. You have taken a major step forward in the lifelong healing process. I also dedicate this work to victims still sequestered within themselves, wanting to speak up but afraid to do so. You are loved and respected for what you are going through. Please reach out to a reputable source of growth and grace to help you begin your lifelong healing process. Compassionate and competent groups exist who will walk with you on the journey toward a better understanding and a brighter outlook.

Table of Contents

Acknowledgements

I would like to extend my thanks to my brothers and sisters at Everyday Fellowship for their prayers and emotional support.

I could not have accomplished this work were it not for the members of the Truth and Restore FCCF group, who logged, recorded, and archived an immense amount of information and documentation. Thank you, RestoreFCCF.org Web Administrator, for making that available for me to access six years after the fact.

My hat also goes off to the whistleblowers for taking a stand for the victims and for not backing down. I am grateful for their encouragement to put my story into words and for giving me permission to quote them.

I am unspeakably grateful to God, who, through his Holy Spirit, prompted me to write my account. I am also thankful for the conviction by the Holy Spirit to keep me moving forward on this project. Some days were too intense to proceed, but his loving kindness drew me back to the keyboard whenever I wanted to turn away.

Foreword

When I finished my thesis on the history of the First Christian Church of Florissant, it was far and away one of the greatest sources of pride in my professional life. FCCF, as it was colloquially called in those days all around the Saint Louis metro area, was a shining example of everything that was good about the independent Christian churches in the region. It had a long history of solid, skilled leadership. Charles Wingfield had served faithfully for the better part of four decades and though an imperfect man, he'd never made a big mistake. The end result was a church that had grown slowly and steadily along with greater North Saint Louis County. Even when population growth slowed, the church continued to expand. Everything was up and to the right for FCCF.

The Church was an active family church. People flocked there not only on Sunday mornings, but also on Sunday nights and midweek for worship gatherings, children ministry, and student programming. Word of mouth in the community brought more and more families to the congregation. Along with Harvester Christian Church in Saint Charles and a couple others, First Christian Church of Florissant was a poster child for ministry success.

I had researched the history diligently, often in awe of it all. I also had had a front-row seat. Since arriving in Florissant for college in 1999, I'd attended sporadically and had friends who volunteered there. Starting in 2001, I worked part time at the church in the student and college-age ministries. In 2003 I landed a full-time, year-long internship. And, after a brief stint doing ministry elsewhere, I returned to FCCF in 2005 on the staff full-time. In addition, my wife grew up at FCCF, finding the church through a friend of her mother's and, from sixth grade on, being active in the student ministry and singing on the worship team. I had a long list of personal stories to bolster my opinion of the church's positive impact in the community, all of which I marveled at in producing my paper.

So, when I completed and published my thesis, I was proud of what I'd written and provided to the community of Christian churches all across America. It was a good story – a story worth celebrating. It was news people needed to hear. For fifty years, the church had been a shining light for the community and benefited countless lives – my own included. My exuberant thesis went to press in the summer of 2008.

Just three short years later, in June 2011, I was packing a moving truck to leave. For the better part of the past two years, I'd watched as everything I'd celebrated about the congregation frayed at its seams. Because of my great love for the congregation, I'd stuck around and tried to redeem some of the wrongs. I did not handle everything perfectly in those years – I was in my late 20s, after all – but I had done my best to speak the truth in an open and honest way. Through a long series of disagreements, I had grown completely disgruntled. Because of the love I held for the congregation I had stayed for nearly two years in this state of dissatisfaction. I really believed I could help change things. But I could not. So, I left, moving my family to Texas.

I wasn't alone. Hundreds of folks and about two-thirds of the staff left over the span of 2-3 years. I was not the first to abandon ship, nor was I the last. The face of the church changed dramatically from 2009-2012. In the years that followed my departure, a large chorus of former FCCF congregants jokingly asked me when I would write the sequel to my thesis. Glowing, positive, celebratory – they felt the first edition was in need of a follow-up that told the rest of the story. What happened, everyone wondered aloud, to the church they loved? What went wrong? These questions continued as more staff left, as more of the congregation scattered, as more people became disenchanted with the place that had once been the center of their lives. They were all right, of course. And they were grieving, because something beautiful had been lost. I shared in this grief from afar.

I have nostalgic, warm feelings associated with the Thanksgiving Eve service in the FCCF lobby. The laughter and love present in that place was impactful to literally thousands of people over the years. I had dedicated both of my children there. I'd been married there. I had been given opportunities to lead that connected me to hundreds and hundreds of students and their families. For pretty much all the 2000s, every holiday my family celebrated was spent there. I played John the Baptist in the Easter pageant. My wife sang on the worship team. The memories go on and on. It wasn't just a church. It was a family.

Now, the diaspora of former FCCF family reached every corner of the Saint Louis area. My best friends, people who I served on staff with for years, left for other ministries all over the United States.

It wasn't just that we'd all left a place – it was that the place we lovingly remembered wasn't even there anymore. Something drastic had changed. Something had really shaken the congregation at its core. And, in their greatest time of need, the people who pledged to protect the church – that is, the people -- protected the institution instead. Congregants scattered, hurt and harmed and hard-pressed to explain the reason why.

What had happened to FCCF?

It's a story worthy of a sequel – but the unpleasantness of it all gave me pause. Even though the questions were jokes, I considered writing it. But I couldn't manage to put pen to page. Life in Texas was busy. I didn't really want to engage in the conflict again. And, truthfully, I knew it would hurt too much to revisit.

I am so thankful that my friend Joy Taylor summoned the strength and courage to compose the answer to that question. What you are about to read is the answer to what happened at First Christian Church of Florissant. Joy has composed a well-researched account of, unfortunately, the darkest days of the church's history. She did so with integrity. This is not a half-cocked, nefariously intended tell-all. It weaves in her personal account with copious research. You can trust what you're reading is the truth, even when the truth hurts.

It is important that we have this at our disposal. To understand FCCF we need to know the stuff worth celebrating and the shadowy side of the church's life. What you're holding in your hands is essential for more than simply localized lesson-learning. This book has a broader importance. It plays out like the wildly popular podcast, *The Rise and Fall of Mars Hill*, which traced the rise and fall of a prominent church in the Pacific Northwest. It is time for all Christians to take a long, hard look in the mirror at the congregations they call home. There are pervasive issues infecting Christianity at a base level. Ignoring them doesn't make them go away. We have to engage.

This book is an invitation to do just that. It gives us the opportunity to discern where to go from here. What you are about to read is not a happy story – but it can still be a good story. It can prevent another place from making similar mistakes. Only when we acknowledge them can we redeem them. Only when we admit our failures can we cease making the same mistakes over and over again.

A wise reader of this book can digest the difficult narrative and grow resolute in helping to change that narrative. I hope you read it with that motivation in mind, because that's the motivation with which Joy composed it.

I'm grateful to her for that.

Titus Benton
Katy, Texas

Chapter 1: The Prelude

Who can forget the eyes of their abuser? My head jolted forward and then lifted backwards as the T-shirt ribbing strafed my neck. He tore the shirt from me, and his hands pushed hard against my shoulders, forcing me to fall backwards onto the bed. Then he jumped with both knees landing on my chest. I let out a reverse gasp pushed from my lungs with the weight of his landing. I searched his face, leering over me. I had never seen that expression in all our married years. Before I knew it, he raised his hand and slapped my face twice, hard enough to leave the smarting imprint of his palm. Did he say something in the intervening seconds? Did I ask him to stop? I can't recall, but I can still see his eyes and his threatening figure towering over me. These were not the eyes of the man who supposedly loved me. These eyes intended to harm me.

It wasn't the first physical encounter but one of several during our marriage. It wasn't the worst of those encounters either, the others leaving bruises and scars, but it was a watershed moment. It was the last of them.

I'm a conflict avoider. I spent almost thirty-four years in a conflicted marriage avoiding the issue, and I'm not proud to say that I also contributed my share of the problems. Conflict avoided rehashes itself and escalates into abuse or violence. That's what happened in my marriage. The conflict I avoided followed me. The more I tried to duck it, the greater the target I became until, in my effort to stay clear of the fray, I stopped speaking back to the tirades against me. Strangely, that didn't stop the fights; it just made them one sided. Not defending myself in the messiness caused me to lose my voice and my ability to make a stand for what I thought was right. I kept thinking that things would change if I was the right Christian wife for my husband. After all, he kept pounding me into submitting. Oh, there's that offensive word, submission. He used it as a weapon in many an argument. I tried to reconcile Scripture to my reality and bring myself back to sanity, but whenever I got back up, he pushed me down over and over again until I internalized the message. I began to believe the lie that twisted God's Word.

I tried to ground myself, to write lists of the Scriptural attributes of a good husband and a good wife. We attended church but mostly after huge blow-ups. The idea was not to make ours a godly union but to correct my attitude and, therefore, save our marriage.

We didn't talk about how we could work together to solve our recurrent battles. I was the reason they happened — something I did, something I didn't do, something I said, something I didn't say. If a fight was on the docket for the day, there was nothing I could do to stop it. All those years went by with us swirling around each other like the Tasmanian devil in the cartoons. One final physical confrontation sent us into counseling, but the fabric over the knees of our relationship was too frayed and the tender skin beneath too scarred. Our divorce became final in June 2003.

The turmoil of the legal proceedings left me physically, emotionally, and financially spent. I refinanced the house to put it in my name, but I barely qualified, my credit rating in shambles. Yet, the wrangling ended, and peace returned, little by little. I found myself grieving the loss but not of our marriage. I mourned the dream of being loved because I came to the tragic conclusion that what was between me and my now ex-husband was far from any sane definition of love. It was a hard realization. Like a middle-school student moving into high school, I was forced into starting over, redefining who I was and where I wanted to go. The voiceless me with the downtrodden spirit had to find a way to keep up with my challenging job while putting Humpty Dumpty back together fast enough and strong enough to survive. Part of starting over meant searching for a church home, a real home where I could participate in the choir and join an adult Sunday school class. A family member recommended the First Christian Church of Florissant (FCCF) because of the reputation of the senior pastor and his son.

I give you a glimpse of my situation and state of mind because it played a large role in the unexpected events to come. Some might infer that a history of abuse disqualifies a person from credibly speaking out against other abuse later in life. On the contrary, my greater than ten-year experience in the Celebrate Recovery Ministry showed me that recovery gives the abused party the ability to speak from a position of confidence and strength. The process of recovery forced me to dig back into my years on Earth to find the root cause of my codependency and to recognize it when it resurfaces, so I can deal with it in real time, using the tools I learned in self-discovery. No one truly knows or can speak to what survivors go through because recovered survivors are the only expert witnesses to their testimony.

> I find that there's a chasm that exists between church leaders and survivors. Sadly, while survivors are isolated, ridiculed, and abandoned by church leaders, they see their abusers

standing with those same leaders on the other side of the chasm . . . Too many abuse survivors are cast out of the church because they are deemed "too bitter", "too unforgiving", or "too emotional," and the list goes on. These "outcasts" are beautiful souls who, in addition to being abused, lost their church community and are shunned by the very people who should have reached out with a helping hand. Survivors have been badly wounded, both by their abusers and by their church.[1]

Abuse victims can choose to wear the label and use it as an excuse, or they can work through the effects of the abuse and allow God to mold the ashes of the past into His purposes to help other victims out of the pit. The work is gut wrenching and hard. It requires counseling and a circle of supportive family and friends. The road is uphill and continues throughout life. A church that obfuscates or abandons victims in an attempt to retain members or uphold the church's image makes the climb out of the pit of abuse that much harder.

This is the story of a growing church in America's Bible Belt with a meager beginning and a record of steady growth for forty-nine years until the steady upward climb of the attendance graph began to bend downward and finally broke under the weight of sexual abuse charges against a youth minister who worked at the church on and off for several years. This is a case history and analysis of events. While assembling the documents, writings, and comments for this study, I realized that the issue went far deeper than the last straw that broke the church's back when the youth minister, Brandon Milburn, was brought to justice and convicted of sexual misconduct against multiple victims.

To portray a complete picture, I need to address several categories throughout the life of FCCF. I start with a history of the church from its inception in 1958 through my last encounter at the church in 2016. I discuss its attempted transition from a traditional church structure to a megachurch, the financial campaigns to keep up with the growing expenses, and its race for greater and greater numbers.

---

[1]Hinton, Jimmy. 2021.*The Devil Inside*. (Warrenton, VA: Freiling Publishing), eBook locations 1569, 1960.

Then I turn to the people, because the congregation is all about the people: the sermons they hear, the loyalty to their church home, their attachment to their pastor, and their deep sense of hurt when they discover the truth of what their leaders hid behind a veil of creative stage settings, dim lighting, and fog machines. I ask myself, "Just who are the victims of this saga? Who are the perpetrators, the abusers?" The answers lie deep within the twisted facts. I present the documented information and personal experience, along with added expert analysis, and I leave you to draw your own conclusions.

Chapter 2: The Parish

The History of FCCF

The church started meeting on May 18, 1958, under the name Grandview Christian Church in a small white house on the campus of the fledgling St. Louis Christian College. Thus, began the newest addition to the association of reformed churches in the St. Louis, Missouri, area, along with the new church's bond with St. Louis Christian College. The college offered use of a house to the newly chartered church for $40 per month. The eighteen founding members poured their hearts, souls, and wallets into developing the congregation. Within two years Grandview Christian Church relocated and changed its name to First Christian Church of Florissant. Fifteen years and three congregation-called pastors later, the membership grew to almost 200 members, and giving increased tenfold.[2]

As the fourth pastor called by the congregation, Charles Wingfield moved his family to Florissant, Missouri, in September 1972 to begin a pastoral position at FCCF. Charles D. Wingfield traveled from his family home in Virginia to Emmanuel School of Religion in Johnson City, Tennessee. Charles was highly influenced by his mentor and professor, Herbert Medford Jones, author of *Building Dynamic Churches*. Though his new pastoral position brought him to a church with declining attendance due to a church split, Charles set about doing the job he had been called there to do, and he did it successfully. The Wingfields made themselves known in the community and in area politics, befriending the mayor and finding favor with the local police and fire chiefs. They became proverbial city pillars as well as honorees at the annual restoration church conferences.

Over the years, the congregation grew and moved to larger buildings until it landed in the location I attended at 2890 Patterson Road in Florissant, Missouri. FCCF entered the new millennium with almost 900 attendees per week on average and an annual giving of over $1,000,000.[3] The beginning years of the twenty-first century saw FCCF hiring additional staff members and pastors.

---

[2] Titus James Benton. *Echoes—Reflections on Our First Fifty Years.*(Florissant, MO: Lucas Parks Books,2008),25–37.

[3] Ibid, 91.

FCCF formed a church-to-church relationship with Southeast Christian Church in Louisville, KY, in the sense that elders attended more than one leadership training session there. According to some who attended, Charles Wingfield admired the person and policies of Bob Russell, the now-retired pastor of SECC. Mr. Russell visited FCCF, preached, and encouraged the leadership in church growth. He had taken his own church from an attendance of 120 to over 18,000, and he was willing to help other restoration churches, including FCCF, with the journey to megachurch status.

The ten principles of Southeast Christian Church growth, per Mr. Russell, are:
- o Proclaim God's word as truth and apply it to people's lives.

- o Worship every week in Spirit and Truth.

- o Develop Christ-centered leaders who lead by example.

- o Do your best in every area of service.

- o Be willing to step out with a bold faith and take risks.

- o Maintain a spirit of harmony.

- o Expect the congregation to participate in every ministry.

- o Continually practice agape love for one another.

- o Give generously of God's resources as a church and as individuals.

- o Commit enthusiastically to evangelism as your primary mission.[4]

Several connections resulted from the two churches' relationship, including intern trades and friends bringing friends into the hired circle at FCCF. Thus, grew the ties between the Wingfields and Southeast Christian Church.

---

[4]Bob Russell. *When God Builds a Church.* (Brentwood, TN: Howard Publishing, 2000), table of contents.

Charles greeted members at the door, knew their names and circumstances, and extended his pastoral hand to each one. He was the beloved patriarch of the church. His wife, Ruth, was revered as well. They worked together, both of them on the payroll, to see that the church became all that God wanted it to be and more, working with his elders and keeping a close eye on what it took to claim success. Charles explained it this way:

> The question has often been posed to me: "How do you account for the steady growth of FCCF over these many years?"
>
> Key points in answering that question would be:
> (1) commitment to church growth by the leadership;
> (2) unity within the leadership and congregation; (3) very limited turnover of trained leaders and paid staff; (4) a balanced program designed to meet the needs and utilize the strengths of all age groups and (6) a conscious and deliberate effort to remove all hindrances to church growth.
>
> It was drilled into me by Dr. Medford Jones, my church growth professor at Emmanuel School of Religion, that "God wants His church to grow!" We can sow seeds and water them, but only God can give the increase. If we preach the gospel, which is the power of God unto salvation to all who believe, then remove the hindrances that tend to keep the local church from growing (lack of space, lack of vision, inadequate staff, disunity, or neglected groups or needs within the church), God gives the increase. One of the most prominent echoes in this volume is telling: TO GOD BE THE GLORY.[5]

In Mr. Russell's words, "God doesn't define success in the same terms that we do. Although we rejoice over our numerical growth, we know that God doesn't measure success in terms of attendance, offerings or size of buildings. He measures effectiveness in terms of faithfulness to His Word, conformity to Jesus Christ, and ministry to those in need."[6]

---

[5] Benton, vii–viii.

[6] Russell, Introduction, pp1-12.

I joined the church about a year after my divorce finalized. At that time, Charles was the senior pastor, and the congregation met in a sanctuary that held perhaps 250 people. They did four services each Sunday to accommodate the large congregation. By then the average weekly attendance had risen to over 1,100, and annual tithes were at $2,000,000.[7] One of Charles' guiding philosophies was that growth stops when the pews are filled to capacity. So, bigger options became a necessity to keep the curve headed upward. FCCF was just about to embark on another building expansion by adding a new worship center. The financial campaign was planned and executed over several months with involvement church wide through prayer vigils and giving commitments, including loans from church members, eventually totaling $2,374,000.[8]

Shortly before construction on the new wing of the church began, the elders announced the plan for the succession of pastors on September 5, 2004.

> Recognizing the importance of stable leadership in providing a healthy church, the elders have been planning for the future . . . and have come to a unanimous decision . . . Steve Wingfield has been asked to become senior minister when Charles steps out of that role at some point during the next three years. Steve will be handling increased responsibilities now as part of this transition . . . we're excited as we look to our church's future and Steve's leadership [9].

The transition period actually began in 1999 when Steve presented his proposal to be designated as senior pastor. Steve's move to seek the higher position prompted Charles to reassess his future plans. The team of elders prepared a letter in response to Steve's proposal, affirming areas of giftedness in Steve's ministry but requesting that he gain further experience before taking over as the senior pastor. This push back from the elders indicates that likely a majority of elders was uncomfortable with Steve being named as Charles' successor.

---

[7] Benton, 109.

[8] Ibid, 98.

[9] Ibid, 99.

An unfinished draft of this letter to Steve reads as follows:

> November 1999
>
> Dear Steve,
>
> The elders have prayed, met and discussed on several occasions your question and proposal for transition into the role of Senior Pastor.
>
> The elders affirm your preaching, knowledge of the congregation, knowledge of church growth factors, evangelistic zeal, and your pastor's heart. As an associate pastor in our congregation your contributions have been an important part of our continued growth and we affirm your contributions in these areas. All of the elders agree that we would like for you to continue as our Associate Pastor. We all also agree that we are uncomfortable with a long transition plan . . .

Steve was working on his skills, as acknowledged by the elders; however, "All of the elders agree that we would like for you to continue as our Associate Pastor" speaks volumes. Charles roundly dismissed the letter, and the mantle was passed eight years later. However, realizing the reluctance of the elders, Charles began bringing leaders of other megachurches in to relate their experience of selecting a new senior pastor, detailing to the elders the decisions and paths taken to facilitate their significant leadership change. The advice from the SECC training had been to prepare both the ministry and the church body for an easy transition from a retiring pastor to his successor, which was followed by FCCF. However, SECC hadn't mentioned that a son should necessarily follow into the position that his father had held for over thirty-five years.

Charles slowly negotiated the pathway over the next five years to assure that Steve would become the unanimous choice of the elders to be his successor.[10] The elders appear to have been pressured into going along with not only the ascension of the younger Wingfield, but also the long transition period.

---

[10] Elder #1.

I find it interesting that the elders address Steve on his question and proposal. I would have expected that Charles would have put forward the request and set the plan of transition, as Steve occupied the subordinate position and not the other way around.

Nepotism

The elephant in the room here is nepotism, defined as "from Latin Nepos, granting of employment to family members regardless of merit."[11] From the point in 1987 of Steve Wingfield being called as associate pastor, nepotism was a part of the First Christian Church of Florissant framework.

David Kowalski, a pastor and English teacher, wrote a couple articles on the foibles of nepotism in churches for an *Apologetics Index*, which included the following:

> Though, in the Old Testament, the monarchy was passed along to physical descendants, the New Testament advocates no such practice in church leadership. The apostolic dictate on the appointment of church leaders was that it should be done according to merit without favoritism of any kind:
>
> "I solemnly charge you in the presence of God and of Christ Jesus and of His chosen angels, to maintain these principles without bias, doing nothing in a spirit of partiality." (1 Timothy 5:21)
>
> "The things which you have heard from me in the presence of many witnesses, entrust these to faithful men who will be able to teach others also." (2 Timothy 2:2)[12]

Here is further commentary by Ronald E. Keener:

> It seems that nepotism, which grants employment to family members regardless of merit, is not a New Testament method of appointing leaders or any paid staff. Apart from

---

[11]David Kowalski, "Body of Christ or Family Business? Nepotism in the Church," Apologetics Index, *https://www.apologeticsindex.org/3001-nepotism-in-the-church.*

[12] Ibid.

---

dominion theologians such as Rousas Rushdoony, who favor some form of imposition of Old Testament law, most Christian leaders and ethicists frown upon the practice. In the August issue of Church Executive, a business magazine for larger and mega churches, Robert Cubillos, business administrator at Rolling Hills Covenant Church, Rolling Hills Estates, CA writes the following:

The consideration and hiring of an employee who is closely connected — by a blood relation — to another employee can cause a great deal of concern for churches . . . Nepotism can create a group of people who are insular and self-referential; they are insulated from outside scrutiny and opinion and are allied together by powerful allegiances to each other. Our concern was to avoid any situations tending toward partiality and/or favoritism that threaten our church's organizational unity and our ability to function cohesively.[13]

The Evangelical Council for Financial Accountability, a leading Evangelical organization for the promotion of financial integrity in the church, shows some concern over the practice in its sample policy for churches regarding nepotism.

Policy - XYZ Ministry permits the employment of qualified relatives of employees, of the employee's household, or immediate family as long as such employment does not, in the opinion of the Ministry, create actual conflicts of interest. For purposes of this policy, "qualified relative" is defined as a spouse, child, parent, sibling, grandparent, grandchild, aunt, uncle, first cousin, corresponding in-law, "step" relation, or any member of the employee's household. The Ministry will use sound judgment in the placement of related employees in accordance with the following guidelines:

Individuals who are related by blood, marriage, or reside in the same household are permitted to work in the same Ministry department, provided no direct reporting or

---

[13]Ronald E. Keener, "When the pastor brings the wife and kid on staff, how should a church respond?", Church Executive, March 4, 2010, https://churchexecutive.com/archives/when-the-pastor-brings-the-wife-and-kid-on-staff-how-should-a-church-respond.

supervisor to subordinate relationship exists. That is, no employee is permitted to work within "the chain of command" when one relative's work responsibilities, salary, hours, career progress, benefits, or other terms and conditions of employment could be influenced by the other relative.[14]

The FCCF.org website currently lists the following staff members:

- Steve Wingfield – Senior Pastor
- Ruth Wingfield – Children's Choir Director
- Kyle Shelnutt – Worship Minister

Ruth is Steve Wingfield's mother. Kyle is Steve's son-in-law. Kyle's wife, Lauren Wingfield Shelnutt, lists herself as the School Administrator at Grace Christian Academy, the school that was housed at First Christian Church of Florissant, according to the Facebook pages of Lauren and the school. FCCF has become the Wingfield dynasty, specializing in nepotism in the church. As noted in a quote above "they are insulated from outside scrutiny and opinion and are allied together by powerful allegiances to each other." Three generations of Wingfield family members worked for the church.[15]

The Transition of the Traditional, Growing Church Toward Megachurch Status and Structure

I became a member in 2003 and joined hundreds of others who participated and observed from the pews. The first services I attended were in the small sanctuary that came to be known as "Stage 1." The pews were filled to capacity for at least three services, precipitating the need for a larger sanctuary. So began the expansion project. I was one of the church members who wrote a favorite Scripture verse on one of the support beams and again on the cement steps, prior to the carpet being laid down in the sanctuary. It was like taking ownership of a little piece of the building.

---

[14]Kowalski.

[15]https://restorefccf.org/documents/current-staff-roster/.

I felt like I was part of the process and a member of the family that had overflowed the smaller sanctuary for multiple Sunday services and was now ready to move into the grand worship center, a project for which the church leadership had taken out a mortgage of $8 million. The ground-breaking ceremony occurred on October 10, 2004. The construction carried on through the remainder of 2004, 2005, and into the fall of 2006. The new facility had its grand opening on October 10, 2006. It was a beautiful worship center with an orchestra pit in the stage and side rows of seating that led up to balcony seating. The project included a 12,500-square-foot lobby area that housed a coffee bar. The new worship center added over 65,000 square feet filled with comfortable theater seating and a choir practice room/green room for performances. It was the perfect venue for multiple years of the production of *Behold the Lamb*.

I became a member of the choir, playing a part in the music ministry and all its pageantry. I also joined a small group composed of fellow choir members. It seemed like I was living the ideal Christian life, giving to the church and serving. I started leading in the divorce support group ministry and then branched out to lead in the Celebrate Recovery ministry, eventually taking the position of assistant ministry leader. I spoke at women's conferences and taught the occasional Sunday school class. Truly, I was what every Christian should be, proving my past accuser wrong, right? Wrong! My perspective soon turned "in the blink of an eye," as Scripture says, and I found myself faced once again with the shell of a dream.

To the best of my understanding, from the depth of researching the documents from that time period and from recalling my reactions and ponderings, here is my interpretation of seeing an established church diminish from unwise church policy and then crumble under the weight of the news that a former youth pastor had been charged with seven counts of sodomy against two young boys. However, let me back away from that eventuality for a moment and cover the transition of the church during the eight years between the opening of the new worship center in 2006 and the arrest of the youth pastor in 2014.

Charles Wingfield worked with the Southeast Christian Church advisors, along with hired consultants and a stewardship campaign company, as the church's debt responsibility waxed, and his years as senior pastor waned. Charles wanted his staff trained in how to grow the church. Mentors visited FCCF for training classes; and FCCF elders reciprocated by going to Louisville and SECC.

It was through this interaction with South East Christian Church that Brandon Milburn became interested in attending St. Louis Christian College. He began volunteering at FCCF in 2005. Eventually, Brandon was employed as an intern in 2006 and 2007.

As Charles came to the end of his role as senior pastor, he worked continually to increase the numbers. He so longed to see church membership top 2,000. Though a few years past his original date Charles eventually reached his goal. Church membership rolls climbed to 2,124, with 1,262 in attendance on an average Sunday. Annual tithes and offerings added up to $2,246,000 by the end of 2007.[16] To be clear, Charles was aiming at megachurch status. The Hartford Institute for Religion Research defines "megachurch" as "any Protestant congregation with a sustained average attendance of 2,000 persons or more in its worship services."[17] Though all 2,000 members may have only shown up on Easter or Christmas, the church was closing in on that statistic.

Charles was a celebrity pastor in his own right. He was a favorite at Johnson Bible College and among the pastors attending the Christian conventions. He was awarded and lauded by them. FCCF kept all the statistics. Perusing the formative years of Titus Benton's thesis clearly shows the importance of statistics to the church's leadership. They tracked attendance, baptisms, and the numbers of recorded sermons requested by the congregation, all of which fell neatly into the definition of "megachurch."

> On the contrary, celebrity pastors are created by numbers that measure success, such as growth metrics demonstrating increases in attendees, baptisms, or sermon downloads that convict Christian audiences of God's hand in congregational expansion.[18]

---

[16] Benton, 109.

[17] Jessica Johnson, *"Megachurches, Celebrity Pastors, and the Evangelical Industrial Complex"* in Religion and Popular Culture in America, Third Edition, *ed. David Forbes (Los Angeles:* University of California Press, *2016),* 159.
[18] Benton, 109.

The baton passed to Steve Wingfield, the new senior pastor.[19]

The path was set for FCCF, or so it seemed. Statistics grew every year following completion of the new worship center and its grand opening on October 10, 2006. The church started an aggressive staffing plan, adding Associate Pastor Steve Wingfield, Administrative Minister Steve Ross, and Family Life Minister Dennis Hounshell. Scott Seppelt (2007–2012), who later became the Florissant fire chief, stepped out of his role as an elder and accepted a part-time staff position as minister of evangelism. He and Steve Wingfield worked together to host the luncheon seminars they dubbed "Starting Point." Joe Mueller (2007–2012), a graduate of Johnson Bible College and grandson of one of the founding members, took the position of discipleship minister. Staff members turned over a couple times in the next few years, and growth leveled off.

Steve Wingfield continued in his father's methods of using Southeast Christian Church for helping to grow the church under his newly acquired leadership role. The elders attended training sessions with Bob Russell and two other trainers from Southeast Christian Church who made the following points, in addition to others:

> Leadership lessons:
> - Confront issues & disagreements head-on and early on
> - Delegate and do not micro-manage, and God does not measure your worth on statistics.

Elders and minister lessons:
> - The pastor has to be willing to be submissive to the Elders

---

[19]Facebook post for September 2, 2007, https://www.facebook.com/fcstl1/.

- Elders must have discernment—Elders must know when things at the church are NOT going well
- (The) role of a Senior Minister of Administration - has to be TOUGH, business minded person (typically from the business world as opposed to a Bible college).[20]

Steve Wingfield put forth the desire to transition FCCF, a church carefully grown by his father, to the heights of megachurch status. He began hiring for children's ministry and youth ministry. Two interns came for a year and then left for other ministries. Michael Frost, a graduate of Atlanta Christian College, came on as the Worship Minister (2005—2009). He was hired to push the attendance up as a result of great Sunday performances, huge holiday productions, and big-name artist concerts in the new venue created for such spectacles. Michael completed a previous internship at Southeast Christian Church.

In settling into his new position at FCCF, Michael sat down with each of the choir members and told us he wanted to be our personal minister. Though he was young, he strove to make that happen. A couple years later, one of the two previous interns, Titus Benton, graduate of St. Louis Christian College, returned to accept the position as youth minister (2005—2011) after completing his one-year internship at FCCF and an interlude serving elsewhere. He joined a relatively new hire in Chris VandeLinde (2004—2011), a graduate of Johnson Bible College, where Charles Wingfield periodically taught classes.[21] I got to know Michael, Titus, and Joe through my participation in choir events and through presentations that I did at the church, along with my bouncing many scriptural questions off them. I worked closely with Dennis because of the recovery ministries that were established and operated under the Family Life Ministry banner at FCCF. My view from the pews became multi-faceted.

The Rush for Greater Numbers

Game on! The ministry team came to play ball, and church membership grew. However, I noticed that the desire to pull in more members, see more baptisms, and rake in more tithes outpaced Mr. Russell's advice:

---

[20]Staff member notes from the training meeting on June 16, 2007.
[21]Benton, 91–106.

"God doesn't define success in the same terms that we do. Although we rejoice over our numerical growth, we know that God doesn't measure success in terms of attendance, offerings, or size of buildings."

Stay with me through the details, here, because these are vital players in the ensuing saga. Notice the interconnections of the network building among St. Louis Christian College, Southeast Christian Church, and FCCF. The web knit tighter as these participants worked side-by-side. Though my involvement in the church gave me hints of how the church functioned, I was not privy to the inner circle who worked directly with Steve Wingfield. I saw from the pews the image that the church leadership wanted me to see and no more. Yet, so much more went on in the behind-the-scenes workings of the church. One face presented us with fog machines, entertainment, and soft sermons for the congregation. The other face presented administration changes and manipulative measures against staff members that culminated in unspeakable behavior to maintain power.

Change in Bylaws

Over time, dissent grew within the elders and staff at FCCF. Sparks flew, comments said in meetings met with ramifications, and the church body was kept from knowing what happened, under the guise of protecting the church. The main theme became that no one should ever question or say anything bad about the church. This is a reasonable suggestion in the case of most churches to prevent gossip from decaying the unity of the body. However, a bona fide problem festering requires a well-established path to bring it to the attention of leadership. Matthew 18 comes to mind. Such an approach was verbally touted by the leadership but squashed in practice. Charles Wingfield's admonition to confront issues and disagreements head on and early on lost its application.

Steve Wingfield pushed for a new construct of corporate-like church governance. However, the new structure required relieving the elders of oversight powers and bringing the church under the more industrialized method of staff management. This was the flint that started sparks flying in the elders' meetings.

The elders' meeting notes from October 16, 2010, indicate an upcoming change to the bylaws. A congregational meeting was set for November 21, 2010.

The leadership introduced the changes to the congregation as necessary, since the bylaws hadn't been updated for many years, and they needed to be brought into compliance with state requirements. The effect of these changes dismantled the elders' leadership structure and shifted total power to Steve. Dissent within the elders grew as common ground dwindled.

Notes from the elders' meeting on November 12, 2010, indicate more than a hint of spiritual abuse to bring the dissenting elders into line.

> All of this to establish that the elders, particularly Elder #2, Elder #3., and I are making a mountain out of a mole hill. And he wondered why we didn't bring this stuff up in meetings upon which we said, almost with one voice, WE HAVE TRIED AND YOU CUT US OFF AT EVERY TURN! So, we argued over that for a while, all the time being chided for thinking he chides us. (!@#$????@!!!!) Elder #2 committed to reform his behavior, and I said I would commit to working together with the elders as long as I could observe an effort on Steve's behalf to work with us without taking shots at us. Elder #3 didn't have to repent since he was not up for reelection.[22]

Governance discussion and elder responsibilities notes from Steve Wingfield dated February 6, 2011, state his priority for proper operation and protection of the church. He makes three main points of elder duties: 1) strategic oversight and spiritual protection, 2) oversight of and seeing to the lead minister's welfare (specifically including protecting the lead minister), and 3) overseeing their own board and the well-being of the elders.

It says nothing about the elders' powers of oversight regarding the senior minister himself. Every duty is directed toward the protection of the senior minister, thus removing their role in holding him accountable. It makes me question why Steve felt he needed such a high level of protection if he was the beloved pastor of his flock.

The path toward a true megachurch required the business format to move into a nonprofit corporation.

---

[22] Used with permission from Elder #1.

The final bylaws presented to the church in 2012 included this reference in ARTICLE I to the name of the church.

> ARTICLE I
> NAME
> For business and legal purposes, the name of this congregation (the "Church" or the "Corporation") shall be "First Christian Church of Florissant."

The same section of the 1982 version of the FCCF bylaws reads:

> ARTICLE I
> NAME
> For business and legal purposes, the name of this congregation shall be "First Christian Church of Florissant."

The change is subtle, but it indicates the intent to change the governance of the church to more of a corporate structure, with Steve Wingfield as head. There was also a notable change of his title from "pastor" to "minister."

In addition to the reference to the corporate format, the elders' responsibility to hire and fire staff moved to the senior minister's position as part of the bylaw updates. The 1982 bylaws read the same as the 2012 bylaws for ARTICLE VI – MINISTERS, SECTION 5 – DISMISSALS, except for the following phrase in the 2012 version that gives power to dismiss ministers to the senior minister (Steve Wingfield at the time): "As need may arise, the executive minister is authorized to terminate part-time or full-time ministers subject to review and approval of the senior minister and affirmation of the elders." Who, then, had power to dismiss the senior pastor?

The elder authority decreased again under ARTICLE VII for staff members.

> ARTICLE VII
> ADDITIONAL STAFF
> As need may arise, the executive minister is authorized to hire and terminate additional part-time or full-time staff members (secretarial, custodial, ministerial support, etc.) subject to review and approval of the senior minister.

The original 1982 bylaws read:

> ARTICLE VII
> ADDITIONAL STAFF
> As need may arise the elders are authorized to call additional staff members (secretarial, custodial, ministerial, etc.) to serve on a part-time or full-time basis. Those approved to serve as ministers of the Word shall be added in accordance with procedures specified under Article VI.

ARTICLE X SECTION 2 references corporate structure again with the added statement,

> Except as limited by Missouri Nonprofit Corporation Act, the Articles of Incorporation of the Church or these By Laws, the elders shall have authority to take all actions on behalf of the church . . .

Clearly, the intent was to move the church into a corporate governance structure in preparation for operating as a megachurch. An FAQ description was also put out to inform readers that changes were to comply with state nonprofit corporation requirements. I don't remember a discussion of the implications of the changes before the congregational meeting. We were given a comparative copy that showed new verbiage. I certainly didn't think to ask, "What do you mean by 'in compliance'? What will this change in terms of how the church functions?" This is a concrete example of how the people in charge manipulated what the people in the pews could see. It was a significant lack of transparency to completely overhaul the structure of the church and not bring it before the church body in detail. After all, it was the church body that financed the operation. Shouldn't there be an adequate explanation with full disclosure? Looking back now, I am convicted of my complacency and my complicity in enabling this power grab.

With this vote of the congregation, the church went from being an elder-led body to join the evangelical-industrial-complex churches. Steve Wingfield started down the path of celebrity pastor, and he began by being less than candid with the people in the church who had supported his father's ministry spiritually and financially for over forty years.

Some of the elders voiced disapproval at the way the change to a nonprofit corporation was handled. Some of them left their positions as elders. One of the seasoned and trusted elders explained it this way:

> Sent: Tue, August 14, 2012 9:51:49 PM
> Subject: Re: By-laws Final Draft
>
> Bob, thank you for the thought.
>
> Well, not so. The revisions are not available in the Library nor on the website. Looking forward to seeing them.
>
> Bob, is it the thinking of the elders that an important subject like the by-laws revisions is not worth a congregational meeting to discuss the changes that are not just legal updates?
> These are critical changes and not just slight alterations. It makes me very sad that the group is not willing to submit themselves to a public discussion. This approach with a "vote only" congregational meeting seems like you're hiding something and hoping the folks won't notice. For instance, if these proposed changes in staff relationship to the congregation are intended and hoped to bring an improvement in our potential to grow and reach more people for Christ, then why not stand up and talk it up? Tell us what the changes are, why they are needed, and how they will bring the improvements intended.[23]

The New Governance Model

Steve Wingfield instituted efforts and training to transition FCCF from the traditional church model into a business model based on the guidance of the Carver Governance Model for churches,
which refers to the corporate structure and relationship between the board and the CEO. Perhaps the FCCF training for their new governance structure lacked the important information from the Carver Governance Model documentation that the board (the elders) has one employee (the lead minister) and that the lead minister is accountable to the board.

---

[23] Used with the permission of Elder #1.

Using a CEO, the board can express its expectations for the entire organization without having to work out any of the internal, often complex, divisions of labor. Therefore, all the authority granted by the board to the organization is actually granted personally to the CEO. All the accountability of the organization to meet board expectations is charged personally to the CEO. The board, in effect, has one employee. It is important that boards maintain a sense of cause and effect with respect to their CEOs. The board creates the CEO; the CEO does not create the board . . . If the founder becomes the new CEO, it will seem that the CEO is parent to the board. Boards established in this way make a grave error when they mistake an accident of history for a proper view of their accountability. The CEO role, as such, is even in these cases created and governed by the board (see Carver, 1992).[24]

It appears that Steve misapplied the model to FCCF. In doing so, he freed himself of accountability to the congregation and to the elders. The old way of doing things under the abandoned church model gave way to senior minister dictates that led to friction with the staff, to which the elders could no longer minister. The result was the loss of pastoral and administration staff. Questions from the congregation about the staff exodus bubbled up, which precipitated members leaving as well. A statement from the Truth and Reform FCCF leadership group refers to the bylaws change in their 2015 email to the elders requesting Steve's resignation:

In 2010, Steve began to lead the elders through by-law changes to shift management of the church from the elders to the paid staff, with himself as the senior decision maker. This was to provide a framework to allow for greater church growth. In 2012, with little to no explanation and justification to the congregation, Steve and the elders proposed and secured a change in the church by-laws. The change resulted in a tightening of Steve's personal control over the eldership and all decision-making in the church.[25]

---

[24]https://www.nmc.edu/about/board-of-trustees/agendas/2013/031213-retreat.pdf, 6.

[25] *"Resignation Request Letter to Elders 6-15-15," Restore FCCF, June 15, 2015,* https://restorefccf.org/resignation-request-letter-to-elders-6-15-15/.

Changes in Money Handling

Steve Wingfield announced from the pulpit that the ability to designate where donations would be applied was going away. There would be only one pot of money for all church business. Members could no longer designate certain amounts to missions or certain ministries within the church or to pay down the mortgage. With one well from which to dip and a CEO type of leadership, priorities within the church's finances changed.

On the restorefccf.com website, a Restore FCCF member stated:

> Our Tithes and offerings are no longer designated as to which area of ministry to support. Your tithes and offerings are put into one large bucket that is then distributed as needed to various ministries. Steve Wingfield makes those decisions. If tithes are withheld, many staff members are concerned that they will not be paid. The mortgage may fall behind.
> Ministries will suffer[26].

Change in Missions Support

FCCF had long supported missions. The missions report on the FCCF website listed nineteen missions to which the church gave generously.

We can find much to praise God for in the reports of these mission organizations. And it is exciting to think about the response of our congregation in supporting our missions. In financial support, over the last seven years First Christian has given $1,151,995 to missions. Let's give thanks to God for all He is doing around the world and the opportunities we have to serve Him in this work of His Kingdom.

---

[26] https://drive.google.com/drive/folders/1XBxzL5mdMt30o8yOfRyTk265S3YuYJNp

We began to see long-supported missionaries fall off the list of those supported by the church. Steve started dictating his approved ministries and how much money they would receive. The most questionable example I saw was him promoting Daren Wendell, who ran across the nation in order to provide water to Lifewater International—Ethiopia. Darren began in California, passing through St. Louis on his way to the east coast. Steve decided the church would give a few thousand dollars to his cause and asked the congregation to give as well. Part of the hype included Steve and others joining Wendell on the last leg into St. Louis with a celebration at the St. Louis Gateway Arch grounds.

At the end of the nationwide run, Daren collected $144,000 for Lifewater International, a nonprofit that shows 80 percent of their revenue going to projects and 20 percent to administrative and fundraising expenses. Steve Wingfield promoted the run, establishing a running team and a support team to give out bottles of water and join in a celebration under the St. Louis Gateway Arch at the end of the day. Following his pattern of non-transparency, Steve did not disclose his relationship to Daren Wendell by marriage to a family member.

> Steve Wingfield started attending mission meetings approximately 2 years ago. He told the committee that the elders had told him he is in charge of the funds and that he has been given the authority to give mission money to whomever he wanted. The only purpose of the rest of the committee is to do things that need to be done, for instance, put labels on all the water bottles that were handed out for the Run Darren Run thing.[27]

Changes in the missions ministry committee led to the elder in charge stepping down and other members leaving the group. It became evident they were no longer an autonomous ministry of the church under the direction of the missions elder. They were relegated to micromanagement by the senior minister.

---

[27]Stated by a long-term missions committee member, and good friend, who stepped away from the group.

Financial Campaigns

FCCF members, the pew occupants, became accustomed to an annual giving sermon series through the month of November, almost from the church's inception. Charles reminded us that if we didn't bring all our tithes to the storehouse, meaning FCCF, we were robbing God. Charles' goal of 2,000 members and average weekly attendance of 1,262 came to fruition in 2007. The annual giving that year was $2.25 million, and a hopeful projected growth rate would bring in 2,245 members and an estimated potential of $2.5 million in annual giving.

The reins transferred to Steve, under whose leadership attendance dropped rapidly. By the time the bylaws changed to initiate the megachurch model, attendance was lower by perhaps 150 people per week. What happened in 2013 to cause the spike before the huge decline? Attendance slowed steadily but for happenings in 2012, that had a short-term effect on attendance. A series called "Not Too Cool for the Pool" brought in large stand-alone pools in which mass baptisms took place on successive Sundays. The number of people baptized reached forty, but attendance included friends and family of those who opted to be baptized.

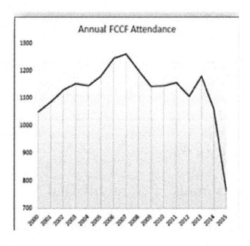

If all families that started in 2007 had stayed with First Christian, our projected attendance would have grown to 2,245, instead it dipped to under 800 each week.[28]

---

[28]"Long-Term Look At Attendance at FCCF," *https://restorefccf.org/long-term-look-at-attendance-at-fccf/.*

The graph shows 2013 marked the beginning of a significant downturn from which FCCF never recovered.

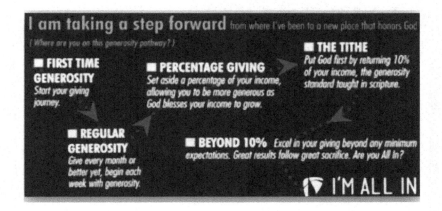

Steve Wingfield carried on the tradition of urging members to give generously to the church, especially, since the expanded mortgage came due in one annual payment at the beginning of each year. The huge addition to the building increased the church's liability and added pressure for greater giving. Although the church had brought in $2.25 million in tithes and offerings seven years earlier, donations did not grow sufficiently.

At the end of 2012, the congregation was shocked when Charles died, but by March 2013, Steve was back in the pulpit with his sermon series, "King of Comebacks." Shortly after that, the ministry team began what seemed to be a year-round financial campaign to get money for needed repairs, renovations to the older section of the church and parking lot improvements.

They called it "The Six Project," a capital drive to complete six projects. The "I'm All In" financial campaign featured the church goals of "reach, win, grow." Leadership asked the congregation to make the commitment to step up in their giving. If they weren't giving, they were to begin. If they were giving, they were to step up to a percentage of their income. If they were already giving a percentage, they were asked to commit to a greater percentage each coming year in regular weekly contributions. The final step up was to go above and beyond the 10 percent of tithing to "Excel in your giving beyond any minimum expectations. Great results follow great sacrifice. Are you All In?"

One of the ideas used to fill the offering plates included bringing old and unwanted jewelry and laying it on the steps of the stage. It was the season of preparing tithe pledges, and, according to the senior minister, the church had fallen behind in the building fund. That is a curious statement because the separate funds had been merged into a single fund only a year prior. Included here is the appeal, as taken from the FCCF website. Steve announced that the jewelry would be melted down, the gems removed, and a new item made by a local jeweler and then sold to add the proceeds to the church's treasury.

I heard later that the jewelry had been made into a cross, but I did not learn of its eventual sale value or even if it had been sold. Within five years the church's financial worries imploded when the church and surrounding communities were shocked by the trial of a youth pastor employed by FCCF on and off from 2006 — 2012. The ensuing uproar within the church caused families to leave in droves. By October 2015, attendance dipped below 800 weekly, and Elder#4/Treasurer recorded a plea for more money and for the members to honor the commitments of the previous year's campaign.[29]

---

[29]First Christian Florissant, Giving Message, performed by Eugen Storjohann (2015; Florissant: First Church Florissant), https://vimeo.com/141827303.

It reminded me of the comments allegedly said in an elder training session about the willingness of leadership to lose hundreds of members in order to gain thousands as part of the new industrial complex model.

The outcropping consequence turned out to be that FCCF lost their building, as they could not make the annual payment on the building's loan. The 2015 financial statement shows a deficit of over $230,000. The $310,000 annual mortgage payment was met for 2015, according to an announcement from the elders on January 27, 2016. The following year, in a letter dated February 19, 2016, the elders reported a 40 percent decrease in funding and a weekly difference in expenses over income by $7,000, resulting in the letting go of three prominent ministers. Eventually, the building was sold to the Solomon Foundation, a nonprofit group in the business of financing church needs. They describe their business as follows:

> The Solomon Foundation is a Church Extension Fund and a registered 501(c)3 non-profit. We offer investments to the people who attend Christian Churches and Churches of Christ, which are part of the Restoration Movement, and provide loans to these same churches, helping them expand their ministry. To provide profitable investment opportunities to individuals, congregations and parachurch organizations and turn them into innovative loans for growing churches" ultimately providing an avenue for greater ministry and expanded impact.[30]

The building was leased back to FCCF in a fifty-year agreement, and now they are at the behest of the new owners as to what is done within the walls that used to be owned by the FCCF congregation. Church staff jobs were threatened. The senior minister's six-figure salary was surely at risk. According to church budgets, Steve's salary was set at over $150,000, which included a $44,000 housing allowance. On the public Facebook group "Help Restore FCCF," a member made the following observation:

June 12, 2015

I've been going through some of the church budgets and something has caught my attention. I see that Steve's salary

---

[30]https://thesolomonfoundation.org/job-opportunities/.

in 2013 was $154,000.00 and that salary included a $44,000.00 housing allowance. Is it normal for a Pastor of a church of less than a 1,000 in weekly attendance to make this much money? Is a $44,000.00 housing allowance really necessary?[31]

The view from the pews during the switch over to the corporate model was puzzling and disheartening; I questioned the motives of my spiritual leaders.

Now is a good time to discuss the pastor and what led to the implosion of a once-thriving church body. I was saddened by this eventuality, but the lack of transparency of the senior minister and the elders throughout the process leading up to this culmination angers me to this day.

---

[31] https://www.facebook.com/groups/1438158796497471

Chapter 3: The Pastor

Steve Wingfield, son of Charles Wingfield, advanced to the position of senior minister of the church in September 2007. According to Charles' obituary, Steve had five siblings: Doug, Melody, Tim, Mindy, and Paul. Raised near FCCF, he graduated from Hazelwood Central High school, just down the road from the church. He went on to graduate from Johnson Bible College in Knoxville, TN. He then attended another local institution, Covenant Theological Seminary, a denominational seminary of the Presbyterian Church in America, located in Creve Coeur, MO, where he received a master's degree in theological studies.[32] He stepped into the pulpit as lead minister with credentials, but did he possess the skills to fill his father's shoes? The church that Steve's father passed into his stewardship was described as follows:

> After a thirty-five-year adventure of faith, a new journey
> was beginning. It was beginning at record-setting pace.
> More people than ever made decisions for Christ — 225 in all.
> This allowed for weekly worship attendance of 1,242
> individuals and a Sunday school attendance of 540. There
> was now a total membership of 2,214 people.[33]

Annual giving for Charles' final year as lead pastor was $2,246,000. Steve took over a highly successful church body that ministered to a growing community, as several new housing areas popped up within a ten-mile radius from the church. His status within the community of Florissant and within the ministry at large may indicate his dream of becoming a megachurch pastor had come true. He and his wife attended the 2015 Megachurch Conference in Florida for pastors seeking to lead megachurches.[34] Steve made inroads and friendships with others seeking to follow the same steps down the road to a giant church.

---

[32] https://www.facebook.com/steve.wingfield.77.

[33] Benton, 108.

[34]https://www.google.com/url?sa=t&rct=j&q=&esrc=s&source=web&cd=&ved=2ahUKEwipp4m 4-YzsAhVJU98KHZ_xDgA4ChAWMAJ6BAgCEAE&url=https%3A%2F%2Fwww.the-meeting-connection.com%2Fmegachurch%2F2015%2Fmegachurch-roster-2015.xlsx&usg=AOvVaw2SczLlBk8RPmhFV4A7Kcty

Charles Wingfield passed away December 4, 2012.[35] FCCF and a good many of Florissant's residents mourned with the Wingfield family. Charles was memorialized at the Christian Convention. Steve had already been in the role of senior minister for five years. I believe the next four years were the best experience and worst experience in the history of FCCF. The church buzzed with greater community outreach through the facility's use for grand productions and visiting artists. Yet, the full impact of the new bylaws that gave CEO control to Steve became disruptively apparent. What perfect storm of events and personalities brought this about?

The years prior to 2007 when the baton passed to Steve, two youth ministers and one worship minister joined the staff. Titus Benton and Chris VandeLinde grew the youth ministries to the point where young voices filled the halls on Wednesday nights. A new youth worship center evolved with all the activity. The addition of Michael Frost not only improved the Sunday services, his production talents created the gospel pageant "Behold the Lamb," which ran for three years, each performance better than the last. Interest in joining the church and the choirs grew by leaps and bounds. Then, 2009 proved to be a point of downturn. The overwhelming success of "Behold the Lamb" that year was partly due to the use of a giant turntable to facilitate scene changes.

A miscommunication regarding selling tickets in order to pay for the production costs became the arrow through the heart of the worship ministry.

Michael was put through church disciplinary measures for something that may not have been his doing. Whatever the case was behind the scenes in the elder meetings, the people in the pews were left wondering why their beloved worship minister was no longer leading. The choir deflated, and several in the congregation left the church in anger at the announced measures. One of the elders delivered the news to the church at the end of Sunday services, explaining Michael's alleged discipline. Though the senior minister led the movement, he used the elders to give the impression of unity among leadership. However, I am not sure that was the true sentiment of the elders.

---

[35]"Charles D. Wingfield," *St. Louis Post-Dispatch*, Dec. 6, 2012, https://www.legacy.com/us/obituaries/stltoday/name/charles-wingfield-obituary?pid=161512879.

Michael dutifully served his penance and then moved on to work at another church in the area. The circumstances surrounding the confusion and disheartening of the church serve as an example of how Steve's management style affected his flock. One of the longtime elders expressed his dismay in an email to his fellow elders:

Tuesday, December 8, 2009, 10:16 PM CST

I had a breakfast visit with Michael this morning to catch up on how he and Amy are doing. I enjoyed the time with him and we had a good conversation. One thing that came up was when I asked if he had ever been asked to meet with the personnel committee privately, without Steve Wingfield present. He said that never happened; he was never in a meeting that did not include Steve. This upsets me. He was never allowed to give an accounting of his activities that were in dispute, when he felt he could be candid about Steve's directives and lack of directives that had impact on his responsibilities. I thought that I had asked whether the committee had met with Michael alone and been told yes. I must be mistaken on that. Frankly I am shocked that the personnel committee did not meet alone with Michael or were not allowed to meet with him by Steve. I see a chain of events that started a couple years ago when Steve transitioned into the pulpit.

1. The junior staff members were barred from attending elders' meetings. We were told that we would have one per meeting come to share the direction of the ministry they were leading. Michael came two different years, may say something that would surprise Steve and then the rebuke at the next staff meeting.

2. Elders were told not to initiate contact with a junior staff member without going through Steve. Also, if a junior staff member contacted us, we should let Steve know. (My sensors are perking up now!)

3. The difficulties with Michael were brought to the personnel committee (was there a personnel committee before Michael's issues?) by Steve and no private meeting with Michael was allowed. (I'm really perking up now.)

Does any of this seem questionable in your opinion? Have we been too "agreeable" with Steve's suggestions for leadership transitions to less participation by the elders? If any one of the other staff had "done" what Michael was reported to have done, would they have been brought before the personnel committee (or maybe they have been and we don't know it?)

I suggested that we have an exit interview with Michael which we did not do. My fear is the same as it was last year when we challenged Steve's leadership. He is carefully controlling the information flow from staff to the elders, and it looks as though it is designed to stifle any negative comments about his leadership style. I believe there is still an undercurrent of discontent among the junior staff, whether mild or moderate. The ones who expressed their concern last fall along with Michael remained silent and let him take the brunt of the scorn from my intervention attempt since I had refrained from mentioning their names to Steve.

I hope these are ridiculous musings, but if there is a train of thought, maybe we should be cautious about the future.

Thanks for listening.[36]

Michael's side of the issue depicted the fecklessness of the senior minister.

I have struggled over the years at times because we were made to feel like we failed over and over again. All I dreamed of was offering a place for people to connect and grow in their relationships. I mean, it was the dream team to make it happen. What a team. But, it just all fell apart. We were honored to be part of so many people's lives during those 5 years. We have lifelong relationships because of those 5 years. It's something I will never take for granted. But I will say, and I even had documentation that I shared with many leaders back then, that showed that I had all the financial records and kept great records of what was spent. I

---

[36] Elder #1, used with permission.

never took money, over-spent approved money, or tried to do anything under the table. There was a paper trail. . .there had to be a paper trail. Steve knew how much was spent and was aware the whole time what was going on. It wasn't until he needed a stop light. . .yes, a stop light for a message prop and I was asked about it on Thursday before the weekend that it was needed. I was told to do what I needed to do to get it there by the weekend. After trying to find it locally (and it didn't pan out), I ordered one from Kansas City and had to spend several hundred dollars in next day shipping to get it. . .when all I needed was some advance notice, ya know?[37]

My personal reaction to the church losing the talent of a beloved worship pastor was incredulity, and my heart broke for the loss of the man who opened our relationship by asking to be a personal shepherd to choir members. When the dust cleared, and a replacement worship minister took the stage, Steve pushed forward in his quest to make FCCF a megachurch in every way. As previously described, the bylaws were changed, and the consternation of some of the elders grew, culminating in several of the long-term elders quietly stepping back from their role as leaders.

The smoke and mirrors of the worship service productions hid the crumbling structure of leaders and the disappearance of some members. June 2011 brought the resignation of the revered youth minister, Titus Benton, author of the historical account of FCCF from its inception to 2008. Chris VandeLinde resigned the following month.

Barb Kruse, a longtime member of FCCF and a one-time friend of the Wingfield family, voiced the question circulating periodically through the congregation as to why the doors to the church seemed to be revolving, and more people appeared to be leaving the church than joining: " But I also have to say that there have been many things said and many things happen over the last several years that we get through a phase, we're devastated, we see people leave, we're upset, we pray, we try and get through it. Things settle down, things calm down.

---

[37] Michael Frost interview, August 7, 2021.

Six months later it happens again. Why? We get the same answers. Six months later it happens again. We get the same answers."[38] Barb set out to contact as many past members as possible. Her findings became part of the reasoning for asking for Steve Wingfield's resignation in 2015 at the height of the largest upheaval the church had seen to date.

> When asked why they left, most cited Steve's leadership style and the inability to establish a working relationship with him as the primary reasons, if not the only reason, for departure.[39]

It is clear that the loss of staff and the loss of members hinged on leadership qualities that Steve Wingfield thought were effective yet backfired when he put them into action. The graph of attendees from 2007 on substantiates a correlation with Steve's leadership style. Two more long-term employees resigned the following year, along with a youth minister, Brandon Milburn. Two years later, resignations seared the congregation with the loss of the new worship minister, two interns, the graphic arts staff member, and three more associate/youth pastors. (I go deeper into this personnel loss phenomenon in chapter 6.)

Steve continued his quest to regain the elusive numbers for megachurch qualification, and he worked hard at becoming a celebrity pastor. He began attending conferences with other pastors of large churches and speaking more about himself from the pulpit than he did about Jesus. He touted the sporty Mustang he bought for his daughter by driving it onto the stage as a sermon prop. He used weights to make a biblical point about his exercise plan. He kept his haircut short but sported a scruffy beard look. He wore jeans and black T-shirts like the more famous online pastors. He set the stage with an industrial look and made sure the lighting was perfect. The worship set became more modern and less traditional, and songs more like singing along with the radio than worshipful praise.

Steve had a video made of himself parachuting from an airplane to promote one of the sermon series.

---

[38]Barb Kruse, "Q&A Meeting with Steve Wingfield & Elders – 4-8-15," Restore FCCF, April 8, 2015, https://restorefccf.org/qa-meeting-with-steve-wingfield-elders-4-8-15/.

[39]"Resignation Request Letter To Elders 6-15-15," Restore FCCF, June 15, 2015, https://restorefccf.org/resignation-request-letter-to-elders-6-15-15.

He also posted a larger-than-life picture of him and his wife on a billboard to advertise the church along the interstate highway. In addition, he created a spot for himself in the limelight of the Lifewater International ministry of his relative, who was running across the country to raise money to provide clean drinking water in Ethiopia. The day's finish line under the St. Louis Gateway Arch celebrated their reaching almost halfway along on their trial journey. Darren had done all the training and ran thousands of miles already, day after day. He had earned the recognition; surely a little of it wouldn't be missed. It was about getting the word out about the need for funding Lifewater International, yet Steve managed to emphasize his small part in the overall picture.

I came across an article by Leonardo Blair in The Christian Post online. In his description of how running a church under the CEO model is unbiblical, he quotes Glenn Newman's book, Move Over Pastor, and Make Room for the Rest of Us.

> "The pastor in that church (megachurch) isn't really pastoring anybody. What the people are doing is they are watching a show on the stage. When there is no service, behind the scenes the pastor is running the church like a business and his assistant pastors are like middle managers," said Newman. "I believe that the elders should be leading the church. Not people who sit on a church board but spiritual leaders and we have forgotten that the elders are the spiritual leaders," he added.[40]

Jessica Johnson dives into the makeup of the celebrity pastor, expounding not only on the personality in the pulpit but also current cultural aspects that might play nicely into the tendency to create a church leader focused more on himself and his numbers than following Jesus.

> Megachurch services can feel like music concerts held in high-ceilinged sanctuaries—the sense of anticipation and spectacle is very similar. However, those who sermonize from pulpits that look as though they were made for Grammy winners rather than ministry leaders are not simply charismatic. On the contrary, celebrity pastors are

---

[40]Leonardo Blair, "*Megachurch Pastors Running Churches Like CEOs Unbiblical, Says Former Pastor,*" Christian Post, https://www.christianpost.com/news/megachurch-pastors-running-churches-like-ceos-unbiblical-says-former-pastor-90374/.

created by numbers that measure success, such as growth metrics demonstrating increases in attendees, baptisms, or sermon downloads that convict Christian audiences of God's hand in congregational expansion. Profit and fame are common denominators that cut across religious and secular divides as tropes of popular culture and innovations in media technology are used to convey the Word, generate buzz, and garner tithes. From the revivals of Billy Sunday to Billy Graham, to the televangelists Pat Robinson and Jimmy Bakker, evangelism and celebrity have attracted audiences in vast numbers, generating monetary gain and cultural influence. However, this essay argues that the accelerated ascendency of megachurch celebrity pastors is best examined and understood in terms of marketing strategy and commodification processes specific to a digital age in which social media and interactive technologies are impacting the identity formation of Christians and non-Christians alike. This analysis demonstrates how relationships between celebrity pastors and their congregants are mediated by cultural and technological shifts as church branding has become integral to evangelical purpose.

She concludes:

> During this participatory branding process, audiences are not passive consumers but active contributors to an "evangelical industrial complex" that thrives on elevating megachurch pastors to media elite status.[41]

Does this cultural metamorphosis lead to narcissistic church leaders? Does celebrity status in the church corrupt the original purpose of service to God's kingdom? Does an online click replace the value of a personal touch from the pastor to the congregants? Does the reward of church family and fellowship take second place to the number of sermons downloaded? Does the devoted believer become a free labor participant in the growth of the industrial model? Is spiritual abuse involved in these types of churches?

---

[41]Johnson, 159-160.

Author and speaker Mary DeMuth provides ten ways to spot spiritual abuse in an article published on September 6, 2016. Within her enlightening discussion, the fifth item in her list applies directly to my questions regarding celebrity status. She surmises that churches falling into spiritual abuse:

> 5. Often have a charismatic leader at the helm who starts off well, but slips into arrogance, protectionism and pride. Where a leader might start off being personable and interested in others' issues, he/she eventually withdraws to a small group of "yes people" and isolates from the needs of others. These ministries and churches harbor a cult of personality, meaning if the central figure of the ministry or church left, the entity would collapse, as it was entirely dependent on one person to hold the place together.[42]

Here is DeMuth's eighth discussion point for spotting abuse. It reads similarly to the issues that the elders had during the period when the FCCF bylaws were revamped to meet the industrial complex version of the church. Steve Wingfield set himself as the main leader that the elders were to encircle. He wrote these church governance expectations for his agenda for the February 6, 2011, elder's meeting. If I understand this correctly, Steve was demanding the elders make sure he succeeded.

> 2. Oversee the lead minister and see to his well-being.
>
> Lead minister serves as an elder on the eldership team.
>
> Lead minister gives a monthly report on his areas of responsibility.
>
> Lead minister gives an overall ministry report (monthly or quarterly?) tracking decisions for Christ, worship attendance, offerings, budget health, and staffing. Lead minister models involvement in personal devotions, evangelism, worship, small groups, and tithing.

---

[42] Mary DeMuth, "10 Ways to Spot Spiritual Abuse," restore, Sept. 6, 2016, https://www.marydemuth.com/spiritual-abuse-10-ways-to-spot-it/.

Elders pray for the lead minister.

Elders protect the lead minister.

Elders encourage the lead minister to on-going educational experiences and conferences to expand his vision and learn from others outside of First Christian.

Elders seek opportunities to affirm the lead minister's family.

Elders encourage an annual study leave and use of vacation time.

Annually review lead minister's compensation.[43]

Mary DeMuth continues her list as she writes:

> 8. Buffer him/herself from criticism by placing people around themselves whose only allegiance is to the leader. These leaders and churches view those who bring up legitimate issues as enemies. Those who were once friends/allies swiftly become enemies once a concern is raised. Sometimes these folks are banished, told to be silent, or shamed into submission.[44]

The process of changing the bylaws to the industrial-complex church in the hope it would grow to greater megachurch status resulted in the resignation of several of the elders who had faithfully served for decades. It was a sad outcome, but the trainer of one of the megachurch sessions for the elders had stated his philosophy something about the willingness to lose hundreds in order to gain thousands. It started with the elders quietly backing away. There was no announcement to the church as a whole regarding the fallout amongst the elders.

---

[43] Taken from the meeting handout provided by Elder #1.

[44] Ibid.

If nineteenth-century politician Lord Acton is correct in his statement, "Absolute power corrupts absolutely," a church leader with sole power over a church body that generously gives millions of dollars to the church stands in grave danger of becoming all about himself and protecting his power and compensation. Do those actions translate into narcissistic tendencies? The greatest Christian trait is humility, as described by Andrew Murray in his writings that point to Jesus as our humility. Written in 1895, his book Humility defines the trait as "the displacement of self by the enthronement of God."[45] What follows is antithetical to Andrew Murray's rendering. David Schrock of Southern Equip discusses discerning narcissistic pastors in his article for Southern Seminary. Here are his discussion points in response to his question, "What hath narcissism to do with church ministry?"

> *A narcissistic pastor habitually turns the conversation back to himself. Beware of the pastor who constantly brings attention to himself.

> *A narcissistic pastor responds to correction with anger and self-defense. Beware of the pastor who refuses to consider criticism or receive correction.

> *A narcissistic pastor is more concerned with the immediate welfare of his ministry than the long-term health of God's sheep. Beware of the pastor who is using the church to advance himself.

> *A narcissistic pastor uses church structures and sermons to support themselves. Beware of the pastor who uses the work of others to bolster himself.

> *A narcissistic pastor is overly independent and unwilling to share ministry with others. Beware of the pastor who doesn't share ministry but instead, puts himself in the center of it all.

> *A narcissistic pastor is often unapproachable and surrounded by an entourage. Beware of the pastor who hides himself behind an inner circle and dismisses the whole congregation.

---

[45] Andrew Murray, *Humility The Journey Toward Holiness*, Bethany House Publishers, 2001, p 69.

*A narcissistic pastor misuses the Bible to defend himself and glorify his ministry. Beware of the pastor who uses the Bible to glorify his ministry and defend himself.[46]

The correct answer is, of course, nothing. The Bible is clear on the consequences of pride. Is that not why Satan fell? Could it be the reason behind the consequences at First Christian of Florissant?

> When pride comes, then comes disgrace, but with the humble is wisdom. (Proverbs 11:2, ESV)

A timely article by Leslie Vernick expresses my position.

> As Christian counselors, pastors and people helpers we often have a hard time discerning between an evil heart and an ordinary sinner who messes up, who isn't perfect, and full of weakness and sin.
>
> I think one of the reasons we don't "see" evil is because we find it so difficult to believe that evil individuals actually exist. We can't imagine someone deceiving us with no conscience, hurting others with no remorse, spinning outrageous fabrications to ruin someone's reputation, or pretending he or she is spiritually committed yet has no fear of God before his or her eyes.
>
> - Evil hearts are experts at creating confusion and contention.
>
> - Evil hearts are experts at fooling others with their smooth speech and flattering words.
>
> - Evil hearts crave and demand control, and their highest authority is their own self-reference.
>
> - Evil hearts play on the sympathies of good-willed people, often trumping the grace card.

---

[46] David Shrock, "7 traits of a narcissistic pastor," Southern Equip, October 16, 2020, https://equip.sbts.edu/article/7-traits-of-a-narcissistic-pastor/.

- Evil hearts have no conscience, no remorse.

- They want you to believe that:

- Their horrible actions should have no serious or painful consequences.

- That if I talk like a gospel-believing Christian I am one, even if my actions don't line up with my talk.[47]

Think back on these traits as we move further along the storyline of this broken church. I am not a psychiatrist, nor do I play one in selfies and live videos, and, I want it to be clear that I am not making a diagnosis. I leave it to readers to see the correlation between the research I present and the people and events at FCCF.

FCCF's story was not a new one in 2015. Several celebrity pastors faced accusations of bullying, spiritual abuse, and other abusive and coercive leadership styles in that year and years following. These names include Mark Driscoll, Steve Timmis, Bill Hybels, Tony Antrovegian, Perry Nobel, Ted Haggard, Carl Lentz, James McDonald, Darin Patrick, and Ravi Zacharias. Was Steve Wingfield infected with this epidemic among megachurch pastors? Did absolute power corrupt absolutely in each case, or were these men predisposed through narcissistic personalities to jump at these opportunities? Is the organizational setup of the corporate-style industrial-complex church to blame? Perhaps the truth lies somewhere in the combination of all three. In her blog for Christianity Today, Kate Shellnutt succinctly sums up the behavior pattern:

> "Fifteen people who served under Timmis described to CHRISTIANITY TODAY a pattern of spiritual abuse through bullying and intimidation, overbearing demands in the name of mission and discipline, rejection of critical feedback, and an expectation of unconditional loyalty."[48]

---

[47] Leslie Vernick, "5 Indicators of an Evil and Wicked Heart," Crosswalk.com, May 19, 2015, https://www.crosswalk.com/faith/spiritual-life/5-indicators-of-an-evil-and-wicked-heart.html.

[48] Kate Shellnutt, "Acts 29 CEO Removed Amid 'Accusations of Abusive Leadership, '" *Christianity Today*, Feb. 7, 2020, https://www.christianitytoday.com/news/2020/february/acts-29-ceo-steve-timmis-removed-spiritual-abuse-tch.html.

So, what do you do if you believe your pastor is a narcissist? Psychotherapist Ross Rosenberg suggests an answer as he defines the narcissistic technique of induced conversation as "calculated attempts to engage a person in conversation for the sole purpose of manipulation, control and domination." Merely engaging in discussion with a narcissistic personality draws you into the tar pit of their methodology to twist your words to make you the guilty party.

> They set you up to look bad.. . .Their power, their ability to manipulate people, requires them to bring in other people into their wrestling ring where they can out-maneuver, out power, out manipulate, out think anyone who wants to defend themselves . . . Induced conversation is the most powerful tool of the narcissist. Induced conversation is what keeps them in control. As long as they can get you to respond to them, talk to them, or defend yourself, then you are in the wrestling ring. The narcissist knows exactly the weaknesses and vulnerabilities of their co-dependent prey...All they need to do is talk to you. Do not underestimate the power of the conversation.[49]

Keep this information in mind as you learn about the reactions of the senior minister and his elders to questioning by his congregation as to how he handled the Brandon Milburn revelation.

---

[49]Ross Rosenberg, When You Unmask a Covert Narcissist, RUN, But Quietly! Counterfeit Relationship. Narcissism Expert, performed by Ross Rosenberg (May 30, 2016), YouTube, https://www.youtube.com/watch?v=3an9crV9feM.

Chapter 4: The Perpetrator

Now it's time to bring you up to speed on another character in the saga, the perpetrator, Brandon Milburn, who hailed from Louisville, KY. He was raised within a two-parent Christian family, attending South East Christian Church (SECC). His skinny-jean-clad frame graced the halls there for several years. His mother worked as a buyer/merchandiser at SECC. Brandon's father served in leadership at SECC. Brandon served together with Michael Frost at a summer camp. Michael interned there and was later hired as the worship minister at First Christian of Florissant. The two eventually served together at FCCF when Brandon came to Florissant to attend St. Louis Christian College in 2005. Brandon took classes at the college and worshiped with FCCF, where he volunteered with the youth. He arrived with his striking blue eyes, short blonde hair, and pierced ears, bringing amazing musical and graphic arts talents. He captivated the teens, who swarmed around him as he entered the sanctuary for services. He wooed the congregation from the stage with his vocals and keyboard skills, wearing his bandana, skullcap, or ball cap. He became a favorite, and Steve Wingfield allegedly touted his talents as far above other staff members.

> The church hired Brandon part-time as a children's intern with two other interns the next year (2006), working with 5[th]graders. He would continue as a paid intern through December of 2007.[50]

Brandon graduated from SLCC with an associate degree in December 2007. He moved back to Louisville and began working as a media technician at SECC, where he was employed from January 2008 to April 2009. In August 2009, Brandon's itchy feet brought him back to Florissant and SLCC. He intended to work toward a bachelor's degree in preaching. The following summer, the ever-restless Brandon interned in California at Discovery Church, Simi Valley. The end of the 2010−2011 school year saw Brandon graduate with a bachelor's degree in preaching. FCCF hired him as creative elements director, and he maintained that position until January 2012.

---

[50] Douglas Lay and Titus Benton."Is it Enough?", 2.

Brandon left the employ of FCCF to begin working for Gateway Christian Church in Des Peres, MO, with the blessing of Steve Wingfield. He was hired to produce the graphic arts and run sound for worship services by the worship minister, who turned out to be a fellow SLCC graduate and future son-in-law to Steve Wingfield. While working at Gateway Christian Church on Sundays, Brandon continued to volunteer with the FCCF youth until May 2012. Though no reason was given for Brandon's exit from FCCF at the time of his leaving in January, he made the following statement in a March 18, 2012, text that he allegedly sent to the mother of one of the boys in his youth group, "His parents told me how they were surprised I was fired from FCCF for accusations against me regarding teen boys."[51]

Once again, Brandon was on the move, this time to Mission Church in Ventura, California, in May 2012. It is not clear if he was employed there or merely volunteered for them. FCCF leadership sponsored a dessert send-off for Brandon at which many members of the congregation, me included, brought cards of well wishes and donated funds for Brandon's new cause. I doubt anyone in the congregation suspected anything but trustworthy motivations on behalf of their previous Creative Elements director. Little did we know the truth behind the smoke and mirrors. Brandon moved one more time to a different California church. He was hired by Real Life Church in August 2013. This was the last place he lived prior to his arrest in St. Louis on February 7, 2014. Sometime in 2013, Brandon enrolled in a counseling program with Dr. John Walker in Colorado, according to Douglas Lay's courtroom notes.[52]

Allow me to chronicle the dates more succinctly.[53]

- August 2011 –FCCF hired Brandon as the Creative Elements director. FCCF conducted a mission trip to Joplin, MO, following a tornado that hit the area.

---

[51] Ibid, 14.

[52]Ibid, 6.

[53] Sources for this timeline are https://drive.google.com/drive/folders/1yDjRyc0kwHL-zbIr_mKIyBAt_jZzqli9 and "Is it Enough?" by Douglas Lay and Titus Benton, cited earlier and reprinted in full in the Appendix.

- At least two of the chaperones on that trip reported inappropriate behavior on the part of Brandon with one of the boys to Steve Wingfield.[54]
- January 2012 –FCCF terminated Brandon's employment but allowed him to keep working with the youth groups. Gateway Christian Church hired Brandon as a contract employee on the recommendation of Steve Wingfield. February 2012 – The pastor at Gateway Christian Church contacted Steve Wingfield to report allegations of Brandon's suspicious behavior. The two discussed comments made to by a parent concerned with how much time her son was spending with Brandon and by a student sponsor from FCCF.
- March 18, 2012– Brandon emailed the mother of one of his young students asking permission to continue to befriend the boy.
- February to June 2012– Brandon volunteered with the FCCF youth, including helping to lead vacation Bible school at First Christian.
- May 2012– FCCF celebrated Brandon with a send-off reception as he moved on to a new position at Mission Church in Ventura, California for which he received a recommendation from Steve Wingfield.
- August 2013– Brandon began serving at Real Life Church in Valencia, California. I do not know if he was an actual employee of the church or if he was a volunteer.
- February 2014– Police officers arrested Brandon on seven counts of sodomy against two minor boys as he returned to St. Louis to attend a friend's wedding.

The blonde, blue-eyed, skinny-jean-clad young man with exceptional musical and artistic talent stood face-to-face with law enforcement and the stark décor of a county jail cell. The judge set Brandon's bail at $100,000. Multiple news stories spread Brandon's mug shot across their hard-copy papers and websites. FCCF responded with a press release of its own on February 11, 2014.

---

[54] Lay and Benton, 5;
http://blogs.riverfronttimes.com/dailyrft/2015/05/first_christian_church_of_florissant_brandon_milburn.php.

To our church family,

We have become aware of an arrest and legal charges that
have been made against an individual who was a part of the
church in the past. For the last several years he has been
living in another state. These charges point to 2007 a time
when as a college student, the individual served in a part
time role as an intern. He, as all employees and volunteers
who work with our youth, passed a background check. We
have a justice system that is doing a thorough investigation
and we will assist them any way we can. (To speak with the
police, call 314-xxx-xxxx) Our focus and our first concern
will be how we can best help any victim heal. Thank you for
keeping this matter in your prayers.[55]

On February 11, 2014, the executive minister at FCCF released a press
statement in the St. Louis Post-Dispatch.

Having just heard of these charges from something that
happened in 2007, our first concern is with how we can best
help any victim heal. The charges point to a time when as a
college student he served in a part time role as an intern. For
the last several years he has been living in another state. We
have a justice system who can do the investigation and we
will assist them any way we can as our church family works
through this.[56]

The events of February 2014 lit the fuse that blew things wide open among
the church body at First Christian of Florissant, but the situation
smoldered for a little over a year. Four of the main players waited and
prayed during that time frame that the church leadership would do the
right thing for the victims, the church members, and the community.
Unfortunately, FCCF leadership failed in all three areas. In reality, it was
also a blow to the elders and pastors, but their choices made the problem

---

[55] FCCF posted their press release on the church Facebook page on February 11, 2014.

[56] Valerie Shremp Hahn, "California youth minister faces sodomy charges in St. Louis County," *St. Louis Post-Dispatch*, Feb. 11, 2014, http://www.stltoday.com/news/local/crime-and-courts/california-youth-minister-faces-sodomy-charges-in-stlouis-county/article_3d3299f1-cd97-56d4-baf9-d63e5572efe6.html.

bigger, and the beach ball they tried to keep underwater burst through the surface tension.

- January 26, 2015 –Brandon pleaded guilty to seven counts of statutory first-degree sodomy.
- March 30, 2015–Brandon stood for sentencing of twenty-five years for each count against him, to be served concurrently.

Danny Wicentowski records Prosecutor Michael Hayes' statement to the court at Brandon's trial in his Riverfront Times article, "A Youth Minister's Downfall is Tearing First Christian Church of Florissant Apart," published on May 16, 2015:[57]

"Your Honor," Hayes begins, "Mr. Milburn has pleaded guilty to the seven counts of statutory sodomy, first degree. These seven counts represent a pattern of abuse that took place over a period of years, from the summer of 2007 till the spring of 2009. The defendant had ingratiated himself with the victims' families and with the church that they all participated in." And Milburn's pattern of abuse began even before that. According to Hayes, the state had received information about three other victims in Milburn's hometown of Louisville, Kentucky. Those molestations date back to 2000, when Milburn was in his early teens and the three boys in preschool. Hayes tells the judge that these earlier abuses spanned at least six years. As Hayes speaks, Milburn's bald head droops toward his lap. His expression is blank. "This is a pattern that has been going on for ten years," Hayes says. "We know there are other victims here in St. Louis, at least one who has been named." There is more. Hayes cites a former staff member at First Christian Church of Florissant, or FCCF, the 2,500-member north-county megachurch where Milburn worked as an intern and volunteer on and off between 2005 to 2012. The staffer claimed Milburn showed pornography to some students and exposed himself to others. "Your Honor, again, he used his position as a youth minster to gain access to all these different victims," continues Hayes. "In the sentencing

---

[57] https://www.riverfronttimes.com/stlouis/a-youth-ministers-downfall-is-tearing-first-christian-church-of-florissant-apart/Content?oid=2772430

advisory report, the defendant minimizes his activities, his offenses against the boys in this case, and actually denies there are other victims." Hayes calls Milburn a predator, a pedophile who would reoffend if given the opportunity.

From the parents of one of the Louisville victims: "His actions are the epitome of arrogance and masterful deceit."[58]

My intent is not to retry the case but to show the seriousness of it and the ramifications of the shockwaves spreading from it. Brandon Milburn received a sentence of twenty-five years on each of the seven counts to be served concurrently.[59] The church received a jarring wound that divided the congregation and crumbled the very foundations of its megachurch status. The victims and their families are going through a lifetime of recovery because of Brandon's actions.

---

[58] Letter from the parents of Louisville victim #1 to Judge Cohen, Dated March 5, 2015, entered into evidence March 6, 2015

[59] Circuit Court of the County of St. Louis, State of Missouri, Twenty-first Judicial Circuit, Division 1, Cause No. 14SL CR-1101, March 30, 2015.

Chapter 5: The Professor, The Parent, The Pastor and His Wife

This chapter introduces four more main characters who will take center stage as the story unfolds. They are Douglas Lay, Dawn Varvil, and Titus and Kari Benton. Professor Lay was the students' choice for Professor of the Year at St. Louis Christian College in 2015. Dawn Varvil was a former member of FCCF, a youth sponsor, and a parent. She worked with Brandon to reach youth in the Florissant area through a nonprofit organization. Titus Benton worked for FCCF as a youth pastor for almost six years, and his wife, Kari, worked alongside him. They were married in the FCCF sanctuary. Kari grew up at FCCF. She considered it her home church and knew the Wingfield family personally.

What does it take to blow the whistle?

Douglas Lay

I introduce Professor Douglas Lay in his own words:

> I am a professor of English and TESOL (Teacher of English as a Second Language) at Saint Louis Christian College since 1999, a former pastor in Fenton, Mo, and a former missionary in Puerto Rico for nearly 14 years, having taught English for five years at the University of Puerto Rico in Mayaguez.
>
> I was one of Brandon's professors at SLCC and his only academic advisor from August of 2005 until May of 2011. I was also his mentor, spending time with him outside of the classroom eating lunch together, sharing life.[60]

For the sake of full disclosure, Professor Douglas Lay is a friend and a brother in Christ. I watched his story play out in complete disbelief at what was transpiring before my eyes.

I first learned about Doug through my work in the Celebrate Recovery program and passing discussions. He and his wife also taught the adult Bible class right before the one I attended.

---

[60] Lay and Benton, 40.

I met them leaving the Bible study room as I entered many times. At the time I did not know he was a professor at St. Louis Christian College, nor did I have the pleasure of sitting in on one of his teaching sessions at FCCF. Our distant yet cordial relationship changed upon my receiving a copy of his account of events, entitled "Is it Enough?" The whistle had been blown weeks before I received my copy. Doug sent it through the proper chain of command at the church until it reached my area, the deacons. I assumed that office only a few months earlier via congregational vote. Deacons were pretty much relegated to planning and logistics for church events like the church's Trunk or Treat fall festival.

A man of character and integrity, Prof. Lay (as he is fondly known by his students) walked into a quagmire of sexual abuse perpetrated by Brandon Milburn against two boys from the youth group at FCCF. Doug built a seventeen-year legacy, teaching classes and counseling students with whom he formed lasting relationships. He was chosen by SLCC students as Teacher of the Year for 2015. The striking difference between this man and the FCCF leadership stems from Doug's efforts to bring truth to light while the elders and senior minister sought to silence the truth and cover up the fact that Brandon's predatory behavior was allegedly known by Steve Wingfield but not reported to authorities, as required. Professor Lay's courage in standing up for the victims of the abuse and for the whistleblowers cost him dearly. The personal fallout for Professor Lay and his family, along with the pressure and innuendo leveled against them and the rest of the whistleblowers broke my heart, and the injustice deeply angered my soul. I could no longer just sit in the pews and watch.

Let's dig one layer deeper into the shared interactions of the players. St. Louis Christian College hosted the seedling First Christian Church until it outgrew the little house on campus grounds. The prospering church became a large financial supporter of the school. Some of the church staff members taught at the college. Many of the students at the college attended FCCF. Over twenty FCCF members—elders, Sunday school teachers, and others with family ties to FCCF members—held positions at the college. Conversely, administrators, board members, deans, and interns from SLCC participated at FCCF. St. Louis Christian College garnered financial support from the church revenue and possibly also from individual church members.

The college feared loss of income from prominent area churches because of the exposure.

First Christian Church was one of the largest donors to SLCC. Another church in south St. Louis was led by Steve Wingfield's brother, who threatened to withdraw his church's financial support of the college. The president of the college deflected the pressure. Instead of standing for justice for the victims, these three entities chose to protect their territory and power structure. They chose silencing truth over-exposing evil. They chose their pocketbooks over the victims' welfare. They chose to seek the worst for their brother in Christ in order to silence his voice. Yet, Prof. Lay continued to speak out on behalf of the victims to get them counseling, to help the church react properly to the predator in its midst, and to help protect children in the church from future threats.

"Is it Enough?" broke down the timeline and shed light on the dual nature of the church leadership. Instead of embracing the challenge to openly communicate with the authorities and the church body, the church leaders brought a defamation lawsuit against the whistleblowers to shut them up or make them pay $25,000 in damages. They filed the suit not only in the name of the senior minister and elders but also in the name of the church membership. They sued a church member, making him both a defendant and a plaintiff in the case. Doug explains his dilemma in speaking truth to power in an email response to the president of the college:

> This situation is and has been profoundly heavy not only on my heart and my family, but on many others. I would in no way purposefully attack or destroy the reputation of the school. In fact, as you have said, this is about me and the church I attend. I understand the connections between the school and the college. But I have wondered who or how or why this request was presented. It speaks of an attempt by the elders to try to constrain me to not speak openly.[61]

He further describes the irony of his situation and his reasons for not signing the tainted contract for another year of teaching at the college. Professor Lay gave up his position and salary at the college in his effort to stand for his principles and being forthright instead of two-faced. For the sake of justice and his advocacy on behalf of the victims, Prof. Lay walked away from his legacy at the college. He puts it this way:

---

[61]Douglas Lay, *The Irony of Teaching Truth*, (Create Space November 5, 2015), p. 79.

This was a "complex issue" because the lawsuit also listed the entire FCCF church as plaintiffs in the suit — including the business administrator, the academic dean, the cafeteria director, two adjunct professors, a current college trustee and numerous college students — all as members of FCCF! In fact, I was not only a defendant but also a plaintiff in the lawsuit since I was a member of FCCF.

... the day after the church dropped the lawsuit, the college president and academic dean demanded I thank the elders for dropping the lawsuit and required I apologize to them. Again, why was my employer making demands on me not related to my job responsibilities or performance concerning a personal matter between my church and me?

Is it not obvious that the college president silenced me because of pressure, directly and indirectly, from the leading financial supporting church where I had accused its senior minister of lying and covering-up allegations of sexual abuse by a convicted child molester who was a former employee of the church and a graduate of the college?

The college chose to place disciplinary restraints on a professor for speaking out for truth against the church's mishandling of sexual abuse allegation that directly led to his resignation from the very college where, for 16 years, he was expected to speak the truth when educating Christians to graduate leaders. How ironic! I spoke truth against a leading supporting church of the college, and I lost my teaching career at the college — the irony of teaching truth![62]

Professor Lay was not without support from several brothers and sisters at FCCF, along with his students at SLCC. The Facebook response below expresses a prayer from a former student.

May 3, 2017

Jesus is putting this world back together and He's not quitting until He's done.

---

[62] Prof. Lay. *The Irony of Teaching Truth* (CreateSpace, 2015), pp. 82-83.

One day, St. Louis Christian College will privately and publicly say to Doug Lay, "We were wrong and we are sorry." I do not know when that day will be, but it will come. I do not know why such a simple and Christian statement has not come yet, but it will come. I do not understand why Doug's and my public expression of forgiveness was not met with that simple phrase in response, but I know that one day SLCC will respond with apology and some small gesture of justice.

Despite SLCC's refusal to acknowledge their wrongdoing, Jesus has removed everyone involved with Doug's silencing from their respective positions. Jesus has even removed many who turned blind eyes and deaf ears to our requests for justice. One day, the men and women Jesus has tabbed to fill those positions will stand up and say, "We (SLCC) were wrong, and we are sorry." That day will be a good day. That day exists. That day will come. That day is likely not today.

(*The Chairman) and the trustees could make today (or any day) that day if they so choose. They have not and it seems that they will not. Nevertheless, that day will come just the same.

That day may come in the near future. New SLCC President (*) is coming soon, and I hold out hope that we will get to share that day together. But even if he does not choose to take responsibility on SLCC's behalf for injustice which he did not cause and withheld justice he did not deny, that day will come just the same.

Please pray in advance of that day. Please pray a prayer of mercy for Chairman (*) and others who have lengthened the time before that day comes, that they experience God's generous forgiveness (for they don't know what they're doing). Please pray a prayer of hope for (*the new President) and the potential for resolution he represents. And please pray a prayer of thanks to Jesus for creating the day that Doug receives his justice. It is a day that the Lord has made. Let's rejoice and be glad in it. It'll be here soon enough.

Jesus is putting this world back together and He's not quitting until He's done.[63]

After six years of standing for the victims, Prof. Lay continues to speak out against abuse in the church and on behalf of the victims. He keeps putting the information into the public eye, blowing his proverbial whistle for as long as it takes. Is anyone listening?

> Doug Lay
> July 1, 2019
>
> When a sexual abuse victim is victimized by the clergy and he/she tells a pastor, the pastor must weigh the victim's care with the rest of the church's care. Often, the pastor chooses to care for the 99 and not the 1. If the pastor publicly addresses the abuse, the bad press and the uncomfortable feelings of the families connected with the victim and the predator may lead to people leaving the church. So, to protect people from leaving, it is easier to keep quiet, cover-up the abuse of just one victim. Pastors believe it is wiser to potentially lose one (the victim) then to lose the many.
>
> This is why I would be careful recommending victims telling their pastor first.[64]

Dawn Varvil

Dawn Varvil, a former FCCF member, worked closely with Brandon, reaching out to at-risk kids in the community through a nonprofit project directed at drawing unchurched and troubled kids together. The idea for the nonprofit, The Link, was to build a skate park where teens could gather safely. The interaction Dawn had with Brandon to put their ideas into action raises Dawn to the top of the list for seeing Brandon in action with children, especially because sleepovers at her house were common.

---

[63] https://www.facebook.com/keith.kepley/posts/10154332102986556?__cft__[0]=AZXDrQ-dU7kHTl4uRuC_qyPS88jApH_84lGfuvKQpjIxNAbG2qlXIRtAgUd8VOAESyZa7GooH4VMBs mlop1dGyJ9YvG1JsYtLSauL-PxXx3Mew&__tn__=%2CO%2CP-R

[64]https://www.facebook.com/proflay.

At one time, Dawn counted Brandon as a friend and a trusted coworker in ministry. She was drawn by Brandon's skills in preaching and music and video production. She believed in his devotion to kids who needed mentors.

Dawn is someone who personally felt the sting of the "induced conversation" techniques described by Ross Rosenberg in the video cited in a previous chapter, "When You Unmask a Covert Narcissist, RUN, But Quietly! Counterfeit Relationship. Narcissism Expert." Brandon's text mentions his termination from FCCF in January 2012. He began his contract work for Gateway Christian Church, for which he received a recommendation from Steve Wingfield. Within a month, the pastor at Gateway called Steve to discuss allegations of Brandon's inappropriate behavior with students. In February 2012, Steve called Dawn to a meeting at FCCF with him and the executive minister (who left the church in July 2012). He called her to his location, assisted by the highest officer of the church. Dawn attended with a friend, and the induced conversation began. Dawn found herself overpowered by the status of the two men and at the mercy of Steve's questioning. In the end she began to doubt herself.

Dawn went to the Lay home distraught after meeting with Steve and his executive minister. This is a snippet of the summary of what she revealed to Doug Lay during their conversation.[65]

> He stated that even in light of the information I had given him, he would have no misgivings in recommending Brandon to other churches and would readily write a letter of recommendation for him (paraphrased) . . .

> He questioned my ability to objectively assess the situation with Brandon, questioned my emotional state and suggested that I take care of my family and distance myself from the situation with Brandon.

> He stated that he would "stake his career" on Brandon's innocence.[66]

---

[65] See the entire recap of the discussion in "Is it Enough?" pages 8–11, found in the Appendix.
[66] Lay and Benton, 11.

Dawn described her February 2012, meeting with Steve Wingfield to Danny Wicentowski, a reporter for the Riverfront Times.

> There's no known recording of the meeting, but Varvil wrote detailed notes of her version of the proceedings, and she shared her thoughts with Womble immediately after it ended.
>
> According to Varvil, she told Wingfield and Strandell (the FCCF Executive Minister) everything she'd told Womble and the state child-abuse hotline operator: Milburn's propensity to spoon with Rayner, his (Milburn's) history of exposing himself to five other teen boys, his excuse that it was "just playful stuff guys do."
>
> Wingfield asked her repeatedly if she had directly witnessed Milburn molest any of her sons, Varvil says. She answered no each time.
>
> "Steve told me, basically, that he thought I needed mental help," says Varvil. "He said I was obviously overly involved, overly upset and that I should just be worrying about my own family, not worrying about what Brandon was doing. At that point I was so confused. I thought, 'Well, maybe I am overreacting to everything.'"
>
> After hours of questioning, Varvil left the meeting more uncertain than ever. She spoke to Womble, and then decided to drive to the home of Doug Lay, who by now had developed his own nagging suspicion that something was not right with his former student. At Lay's house, Varvil unloaded the full story. Sobbing, she described everything she had seen of Milburn to Lay and to his wife, and what happened at the meeting earlier that day. The Lays were horrified. They tried to reassure Varvil that she did the right thing.
>
> "Dawn was shattered," Doug Lay says. "She told us everything, and then she said, 'Do you think I'm crazy?'"[67]

---

[67] Wicentowski, May 19, 2015.

Dawn's meeting with the two ministers at FCCF occurred near the second anniversary of Brandon's arrest. About fifteen months later, Dawn was served with the Wingfield/FCCF petition to silence any public discussion of the matter.[68]

Lily Fowler of the St. Louis Post-Dispatch described it this way:

> The civil suit, filed April 16 in St. Louis County Circuit Court, alleged that the months after Milburn's guilty plea saw an escalating pattern of "harassment" directed at Wingfield by those who said he had failed to act on a 2012 conversation with Dawn Varvil, a member of the church who had met with the pastor over concerns she had about Milburn.
>
> Wingfield says Varvil is a liar— and he's seeking a court order to force her to recant the claims about the 2012 meeting. Filed April 16, the lawsuit also seeks at least $25,000 in damages.[69]

Dawn reeled with hurt for a bit, but she came back fighting. As one of the defendants in the Steve Wingfield/FCCF lawsuit, she hired a good lawyer to help her voice her disgust at the allegations and make strong statements as to her intentions to stand up for the victims and for herself. Her lawyer penned the following letter on behalf of Varvil to Wingfield's attorney on June 4, 2015. She did not mince words.

> It is clear from the pleadings, from the falsehoods Wingfield told to witnesses and placed on his website, and from Wingfield's voluntary motion to dismiss (which also contained falsehoods) that Wingfield knew that the case never had any merit. It is further clear that he never had any intention of seeing the lawsuit through.
>
> Wingfield's entire purpose in filing the lawsuit was to harm people who he knew had constitutional rights to speak up for what they believed. He acted selfishly, with reckless

---

[68]http://storage.cloversites.com/firstchristianchurchofflorissant/documents/Verified%20Petition%2015SL-CC01320%20-%2016%20April%202015_3.pdf.

[69]Wicentowski, May 19, 2015.

disregard for his church members, without regard for the good of the future of the church, and with evil intent against innocent people.

Dawn has suffered immeasurably as a result of what Wingfield has done to her. First, Wingfield tried to make her feel that she committed a wrong against the church. He, as a supposed man of God, made her question her own mental health and understanding of the world. As a religious person, this is immensely damaging for Dawn. Next, Wingfield tried to publicly discredit her by calling her a liar in a court of law when he knew he was the one who was lying. He made her pay for attorney's fees to defend herself when he knew the lawsuit was a farce. Lastly, and most importantly, he left Dawn to pick up where he failed. She has been a tireless voice for those abused by Milburn — a voice that was weakened and distracted by Wingfield's lawsuit.

Where Dawn fought for help for survivors of childhood sexual abuse, Wingfield abused the court system to save his own behind. When Dawn made repeated phone calls seeking therapy services for those harmed by Milburn's actions and Wingfield's inaction, Wingfield did nothing positive and instead tried to distract her with a pointless lawsuit.[70]

Dawn laid down her requirements to Wingfield through this communiqué, even threatening a countersuit. She demanded a public letter of apology to all of Milburn's victims and to the whistleblowers. She also asked for financial assistance to provide outside counseling for the victims. She pushed for FCCF to hire Godly Response to Abuse in Christian Environments (GRACE) to review the FCCF policies on childhood sexual abuse and to implement changes and training where necessary, along with establishing oversight to assist families of other adult victims in case more came forward.

---

[70] https://restorefccf.org/varvils-letter-to-steve-wingfield-6-4-15/

She wanted a network of professionals and a victim advocate as part of FCCF's resources. Dawn also wanted all references to the litigation to be removed from the FCCF website, the whistleblowers' attorney fees reimbursed, and dismissal of the FCCF lawsuit with prejudice.

Titus and Kari Benton

Titus Benton became an intern at FCCF in 2003 and served out the year-long assignment. He returned to FCCF as an associate student minister in 2005. Titus wrote a history of FCCF, showing great affection for the institution and for Charles Wingfield, who brought it up from its early beginnings. Kari Benton grew up loving her church. She was baptized into FCCF membership. She and Titus were married at FCCF. The congregation loved them. The couple had their first baby while at FCCF. Titus' laid-back preaching style, through which he delivered solid scriptural teaching, captivated many in the congregation who seemed to like his methods better than the over-propped, self-involved messages by Steve Wingfield. Titus brought the Word and pointed to Jesus. He delivered most of his sermons wearing jeans and flip-flops, which indicated he cared more about what he preached than what he wore. Kari supported Titus but put her own talents on display as well. Her beautiful voice and ability to act landed her parts in "Behold the Lamb" and other choir productions. Kari added value to the church's ministry. She received her nursing credentials in 2006 and is now a nurse practitioner.

The Benton family's abrupt departure from the church made many people in the congregation question what happened. The church leader's narrative was that Titus received a job offer at a church in Texas that he couldn't pass up, and they moved on to a better life. However, my research for this book includes notes from elder meetings discussing Titus' leaving that reveal a different side of the story.

> 1. I'm unhappy that we found out that Titus had been told that the elders were disappointed in him for writing his March letter to Steve (Wingfield). I did not remember that the elders expressed disappointment in Titus for that "insubordinate action." Would this have been the communication from the personnel team on behalf of the elders, or Steve's relating to him on behalf of the elders? Regarding the recent meeting with Titus, I wish we had been told that Titus had requested the meeting last spring or early summer. It was presented as though Titus had called up a

couple weeks ago to request a meeting, whereas in fact the personnel team wasn't able, apparently, to meet with him until recently.

2. It disturbed me to hear Chris (another Student Minister who left FCCF a month after Titus) presented so roughly. I wish the full accounting of the matter of dispute had been given, either by Steve or Scott. We were not told that the programming proposal was brought to Steve's attention prior to his Florida vacation, with an affirmative response. When the details were ready for final review and forwarded to Steve with a request for a meeting to discuss, he had gone to Florida without word to the staff or his personal assistant. We heard the story from that point on. To me, mischaracterizing an issue, leaving out the full account, is malicious in intent, with the intent to sway our opinion of Chris. The fact that Scott jumped on it like he did was further disappointment.

3. Lastly, when (Elder #3) mentioned near the end of our meeting that it would be important for the elders to figure out how we were going to be the evaluators of Steve's leading, Steve turned the question to the "more important question of how the elders will control themselves." I fear that Steve has no intention of allowing himself to be evaluated by this eldership (a bunch of rogues, you know!)[71]

Obviously, the elders were deeply concerned about the circumstances surrounding the resignations of the two beloved student ministers, who had proven themselves to the church body. Why would any church not fight to retain such godly servants? Again, much happens behind the lights, guitars, and fog machines of which those of us in the pews are unaware. The elders' power waned as the CEO-type positioning of the senior minister blossomed from the structural changes to the church business model.

---

[71] Elder #1 email to fellow elders dated Saturday, October 23, 2010, 4:24:35 p.m. Used with permission.

The Bentons left in June 2011. They established themselves at their new home church and became beloved among the new congregation. When the police arrested Brandon Milburn on February 8, 2014, Titus received a call from Professor Lay, who wanted to break the news to the couple personally. Prof. Lay and Titus began documenting their interactions, proving to be true shepherds. They called the victims, talked with their families, and interacted with law enforcement. They were both subpoenaed to testify at any potential trial. Almost a year later, Brandon pleaded guilty and was sentenced in March 2015. Their documented report morphed into "Is it Enough?" which is cited multiple times in this book.

The stage is now set with the cast of characters. The background actors from the congregation, including me, played reactionary parts to what we saw happening. I present my observations, admitting potential biases, yet this was my experience. No one else is an expert on what I saw, heard, and felt while going through it. The many strands of the story weave through the character descriptions so far. Now it's time to tie the threads together and analyze what transpired in the hope of developing a picture of a better way for a church to handle the tragic discovery of abuse within its midst or by someone among their staff. My aim is to present the experiences of two different churches side-by-side. One church chose to push the incidents down the memory hole and move on. The other church chose open and honest communication from church leadership to the congregation. Both churches went through turbulent periods, but the outcomes were strikingly different.

Chapter 6: The Parable

The word "parable" means to cast beside. In keeping with this chapter's title, I set before you two separate churches facing the sexual abuse of children.

Case #1

My view from the pews suddenly widened as the curtains opened to reveal the inner workings threatening my church family.

The morning started out innocently enough with the hated alarm reminding me it was a workday. It promised to be another nondescript partly cloudy March day with a high in the mid-fifties, another cold day, dragging out in anticipation of spring. Like most mornings, I started by scrolling through my Facebook newsfeed, looking for prayer requests to address through my Joy In-Verse Ministry page. I came across an open letter to the senior minister of my church, and the day suddenly became anything but ordinary.

My schedule forced me to wait until I completed my twenty-five-mile commute, culminating in five flights of stairs to call my friend, Celebrate Recovery leader, and Family Life Minister, three titles embodied in one person. All I could say to him was, "We have to talk." At that point I had held a deacon's position under the Family Life Ministry at FCCF for maybe six months. That title came out of more than ten years of leadership in not only the divorce support group but also in Celebrate Recovery. FCCF was my church home, and its people were my church family. I logged a lot of service hours in these two groups that touched the brokenness in us all.

In the Facebook post, Kari Benton called out Steve Wingfield for poor management and pressed for his resignation. Kari was raised in FCCF and was a Wingfield family friend. Kari was also the wife of Titus Benton, who had been one of the youth ministers who left FCCF a few years earlier amidst a series of staff resignations. She posted her letter to a public platform. Here is the section of her post that nearly caused me to spit my coffee across my computer monitor.

> Most disturbing is the fact that in 2012 you were made
> aware by a concerned adult that Brandon was having an

inappropriate relationship with a teenage boy and this adult was very confident that Brandon was abusing this boy. Your response to this adult was basically — That's not true, you're crazy for even suggesting that (I'm paraphrasing here). You failed in that moment. Not only should you have believed this concerned adult, but you also should have gotten on the phone and reported these allegations to the authorities. You did neither. After Brandon was arrested you failed again. The first phone call you should have made after learning of his arrest was to that concerned adult that had previously come to you with concerns of abuse. But you did not do that — and to this day you still have not reached out to that concerned adult or to that teenage boy. You have failed both of them.

What makes this even worse is that this is not the first time you have mishandled situations such as these. Many years ago, another young man was found to have inappropriately touched a younger boy. These two situations are not identical, but your responses are eerily similar. In the name of "protecting" this young man you managed to keep this situation from the public. However honorable you might have thought that was, the fact is a victim was silenced at your request. To me, this shows a clear pattern that when something of this nature comes to your attention your initial reaction is to keep it quiet and to do as little possible in order to preserve yours and/or the church's reputation. In considering these two situations, I conclude your actions have proven you to be untrustworthy when it comes to serious circumstances such as abuse. As a result, if another similar situation were to come to your attention in the future, I have absolutely ZERO confidence that you would handle it appropriately.

It is unacceptable for a lead pastor to be untrustworthy when it comes to handling serious situations such as abuse.[72]

---

[72] https://restorefccf.org/the-open-letter-that-sparked-a-lawsuit/

Was this the diatribe of a disgruntled former employee's spouse, or was it the heartfelt expression of a former long-term church member who knew the back story not seen from the pews? Wait, this was taking place in a church I had attended for more than ten years! How much of a recovery ministry bubble had I put myself into that this would shock me so? Now I needed to ask my trusted friend, the Family Life Minister, what was going on in my church? How much of this did he know? What reaction did he expect from the ministry team? What was the church going to do about this?

The open letter on March 20, 2015, was the culmination of frustration due to the inaction by leadership. I discovered that Titus Benton and Douglas Lay had compiled a timeline of their information on Brandon Milburn because they felt they may have been called as witnesses during the trial. They titled the document "Is it Enough?"

Titus and Doug contacted the elders first and sent them copies of the document to ask for corrections, questions, and alterations. They also sent it to the prosecuting attorney's office and to the sentencing judge, who asked for interested parties with information to present it. The elders' response was a certified letter stating that the church had not taken the role of an investigator. Professor Lay distributed "Is It Enough?" to the nineteen deacons at FCCF on March 25. I was one of them. Doug approached me at church and asked if he could send me the case study. I read through the timeline as objectively as I could, with questions forming in my mind as I turned each page. It took me a few days to digest the information and compose an email to my church leaders, calling for transparency and action. I sent Doug a copy.

The magnitude of the charges and their implications shook me to the core, and I quickly realized the need to take a stand for my convictions. The problem required me to define my position before I could contend for it. I thought I had done that once already, just by the act of accepting Christ as Savior and covenanting with Him to follow his teaching. Now I questioned the church leadership whom I had supported for ten years. So began my foray into the unknown territory of church upheaval. Here is the full text of my email to FCCF's elders.

Joy Taylor
Sat 3/28/2015 11:46 AM

To the FCCF elders:

I'm writing to express deep concern for recent serious and public accusations made against the FCCF leadership. I read the open letter Kari Benton posted on Facebook, and I read the case study on FCCF entitled, "Is it Enough?" by Titus Benton and Professor Doug Lay. I consider all three of these people to be sincere believers who care about honesty and integrity, so their claims disturb me.

There is a piece of the story missing, which is a full disclosure by the church leadership of the events described in these documents. I am a small cog in a huge financial wheel who helps pay salaries for church staff. As I prayerfully come to a decision on what to do with my support in the future, I carefully consider as much information as possible.

As a deacon and a church member, I respectfully request an opportunity to hear your missing account of this issue in an open, honest format before your membership body. I have already been asked about what's going on by some of the members to which I minister in Celebrate Recovery. I would like them to receive answers to their questions in public on these damaging accusations that have been made publicly.

Nothing but abject honesty and full disclosure will do. I can support acknowledgement of the deficiency and solid evidence of positive actions to address the issue through amends to the body and training of staff and volunteers on the proper way to handle threats to those in the body. If mismanagement and poor leadership comes out in the truth of these events, I can support dismissal or remedial actions taken against the individual(s) involved.

As a codependent personality who struggles with the effects of abusive relationships, I get the tendency to cope with negative news with silence, hoping the issue will go away. My personal experience shows me that trying to avoid pain by not removing the splinter only leads to festering and infection. That is where FCCF is today.

It is leadership's role to clean out the infection through open, honest communication with the body of church members that will allow healing to begin. I look forward to participating in a full disclosure meeting of the body, at which your side of the story is told and your positive action plan for the future is revealed.

In His mighty hand,

Joy Taylor[73]

I wrestled mentally with the knowledge and glaring inconsistencies before me. Two days after my message to the FCCF elders, Brandon was sentenced. I wasn't alone. The pressure from congregant questions resulted in the elders calling meetings for the teachers and ministry leaders. I received a response from Elder #4 on April 1, explaining the plan for the elders and leadership to discuss recent events and what they meant to the church. The first meeting was reserved for Sunday school teachers of minors. It was held at the church on April 1, the day after Brandon's sentencing. Easter came and went on April 5. Many of the people in the pews who made it to church only for Easter and Christmas services had no clue about the underlying turmoil about to explode within the church and across local news. The second meeting for the ministry leaders and adult class teachers occurred on April 8.

As part of working through my struggles over my next steps, I notified the Family Life Minister of my decisions. Life circumstances were leading me to semi-retire and move out of St. Louis. I had been making strides in that direction over the past year. I discussed the end of my role as a deacon within the coming months. I emailed my decision points to the family life minister.

> Nevertheless, my plan is to continue to support the church as best I can, but my choices are limited because of the single fund. If I want to continue to support the salaries of staff members, I have to also give to the salaries of those I may choose not to support. That is a difficult place to be in. I will continue to attend my adult Bible class and help there whenever you need me. Depending on the outcome of the

---

[73] Douglas Lay and Titus Benton, pp 31-32

meeting on Wednesday, I may decide I can no longer attend services in which Steve is preaching. In that case, I will be in the prayer room at those times praying for the church, the staff, the elders and for SW. I will attend services at which other staff members are preaching. I will continue to contribute my time, work, prayers and funding to the CR ministry for the remainder of my time in St. Louis. I will not give up my membership to FCCF until after I find a church home in Indiana.

I pray that what transpires will soften the hearts of SW and the elders to be servant leaders operating from a position of humility. I fear, based on personality traits I have seen thus far, that circumstances will harden their hearts and embolden them to greater acts of vindictiveness and control.

A group of like-minded fellow church members began growing, and informal meetings among them started happening at private homes. The buzz on Facebook expanded into a buzz in the sanctuary with many wondering exactly what was going on. Professor Lay wrote a descriptive blurb that was emailed from friend to friend, and the issue started factions in the church. Everyone pondered the same points that plagued me. Should I put my loyalty with the church body, which had been like a family to me, and to the church where my tithes had gone for many years? Should I continue to sit under the teaching of a man who allegedly chose to protect his image rather than the victims and the congregation of parents and children?

I received a PDF titled "What's Going on at FCCF: Serious Answers for a Serious Problem" from Professor Lay, dated April 7. It focused on a primary concern regarding what Steve Wingfield knew about the abuse and what he had done about it. The document asked readers to read, study, pray, and find out the facts before coming to conclusions. It also put forth the accusations of the whistleblowers:

> THE CHARGES
> 1. Steve Wingfield, the senior minister at First Christian Church of Florissant, ignored, lied about, and covered-up sexual abuse allegations of six alleged young boys, all minors, by Brandon Milburn. The alleged abuse took place while Brandon was employed at the church.

2. Steve Wingfield discredited, ignored, and intimidated the reporter, Dawn Varvil, a former church member, youth sponsor, and parent, after she first reported these allegations three years ago to Steve and Scott in February of 2012 at a meeting called by Steve.[74]

The document went on to establish the reasons for the whistleblowers moving forward. The church mailed a letter to Prof. Lay and Titus on March 19 after several meetings between them and the leadership. The whistleblowers felt Steve conducted a cover-up of the information reported to him by multiple sources regarding Brandon. The church leaders refused to conduct an investigation to establish or refute their claims and formalized it in the letter.

The second meeting occurred on Wednesday, April 8. I attended, hoping to get reasonable answers to the full disclosure I pointed out in my email to the elders. I expected a two-way conversation to take place. It became evident very quickly that was not going to happen amicably, though the meeting had been dubbed "a family meeting." Perhaps it did indeed go the path of many actual family meetings.

I entered the area normally used for teen worship services and made my way toward the stage. I found a chair in the first three rows to the right, where my short stature didn't hamper my view. Three of the elders sat toward the back of the stage near Steve Wingfield. The newly ordained executive minister made his way to the front of the stage as people found a seat and quieted.

The parents who attended the first meeting took notes of what was said in their meeting. The leaders from the Celebrate Recovery team recorded the second meeting on someone's phone and transcribed it afterward. The transcription provided an opportunity to compare what was said in the notes from the first meeting on April 1 to what was said in the April 8 meeting. The executive minister opened the meeting, and Elder #5 made a statement about how the church leadership was following requests from the prosecuting attorney in terms of making an announcement from the pulpit in case other victims might come forward.

---

[74] https://restorefccf.org/documents/serious-answers-for-serious-problems-4-7-15/

He alluded to advice sought from South East Christian Church that it was the authorities' job, not the church's, to do the investigation. SECC appeared to take the position that somewhat opposed the police who asked for the announcement to the congregation. The notes from the first meeting mention that the church investigation was ongoing, but only two victims had come forward. The leadership's position at the second meeting negated a church investigation, based on the advice from SECC.

The tension in the room heightened because some of the attendees had also witnessed the first meeting, and they sensed a change in what they had been told the week before. Elder #5 continued to list the church's progress in reviewing policies and protective measures to update them and bolster their effectiveness. He moved the timeline forward to the previous month when the open letter hit Facebook and to when the case study made its rounds. In a third 180-degree turnaround, Elder #5 haltingly told us they did conduct an internal investigation.

> . . . week of March we received a case study from an individual that made an accusation about what Steve knew . . . um, yeah, just made an accusation that Steve knew of Brandon's, what Brandon was, was all about and he covered it up. Our internal investigation, okay? We found that there's clear evidence that this is a false accusation. Okay? We believe one hundred percent in the integrity of Steve, our senior pastor. In this matter, that we stand behind him, no doubt. Okay?[75]

The elders stated their case and fulfilled their job description as elders to surround the senior minister and protect him. Remember that statement in the new bylaws for the industrial-complex church? The elders' wagons were definitely circled around the senior minister. Elder #5 nervously continued in unstructured sentences, bringing in arguments about job turnovers and people leaving frequently in work situations as a normal flow of business. I wondered if someone had asked him why the church had more than ten ministers leave within the past few years. The executive minister prayed at the request of Elder #5, and the opened the floor for questions. The executive minister fielded a couple of queries on how the church was ministering to the hurting, whether Brandon's victims or those who were suffering due to other congregational strife.

---

[75] https://restorefccf.org/qa-meeting-with-steve-wingfield-elders-4-8-15/.

Steve Wingfield shifted uncomfortably in his chair and then stood to take over answering questions. He walked forward and took the microphone, standing midway on the elevated platform that served as the stage. He was maybe thirty feet from where I sat, leaning back in my chair, my legs crossed.

Mr. Wingfield gave passing reference to ministering to the hurting and began the topic of what he knew and when he knew it regarding Brandon's activities. He stated that he and the leadership did not know until right before the news of Brandon's arrest went public because one of the victims and his family called for a meeting to discuss honoring the family's privacy. He intimated that two days before the arrest was the first time he had heard of Brandon's conduct with minor boys. We in the audience knew from reading "Is it Enough?" that at least three people notified Steve about Brandon in the 2011−2012 timeframe. A chaperone who went on a mission trip with the youth in 2011 to Joplin, MO warned him. Dawn Varvil warned him in February 2012. The Pastor of Gateway Christian Church warned him in February 2012. The room temperature went up several degrees in response to his attempt to redirect the onus from him for not reporting Brandon to the authorities three years earlier.

Steve circled back to pick up ministering to the hurting. Without being transparent as to how many times he spoke with the families or called to pray with them or helped arrange healing counseling, he shrugged off his responsibility to minister by telling the group:

> We were given the strong counsel, not only by the family that came to us, that we could only minister to those who went forward to the police, and that's what our communication was. We want you to go to the police, then if we can help you minister, we would be glad to. We were limited to only be able to minister to those who say, "Hey, I'm a victim."[76]

At that point I knew I would not see the transparency from leadership I wanted. His statement made no sense to me. I uncrossed my legs and crossed my arms.

---

[76] Ibid.

Then Steve went off on the foibles of social media and getting information from unreliable sources. He made the mistake of not knowing that his audience was in close contact with the authors of the timeline. If he had any refutations to make, they needed to be factually supported and documented at the same level as the case study to show that the timeline was in error. Instead, he took another route in his discussion to return to the issue of not reporting.

> This is not something for us to talk about every week or every month in our church when there's an open investigation. Um, um, that's the police's role and they serve that role, I believe, very well. And I trust, and I, I trust the police, and have to trust the police in that their roles as investigators. Um, I love our church, I hate people that, I hate that people have to deal with the repercussions of sexual sin. Let me give up some pastoral advice. If you have been a victim of sexual sin, or you're dealing with someone who's a victim, now we, we communicate that. If anybody told me about a sexual crime I would immediately hotline and have done that in the past. And you need to understand that there are laws in the state of Missouri of mandated reporting and I am obedient to the law. And if I received an accusation of sexual misconduct by Brandon or anyone, I would immediately hotline that.[77]

After his Freudian slip and changing "hating people" to "hating sin," Steve began to establish his power stance as the pastoral authority in order to give what he said next more clout. It seemed to me that he believed his last sentence made up for the fact that he hadn't reported Brandon in 2012. It didn't. It didn't make up for it for me, and it didn't make up for it to others either, judging by the reactions amongst the crowd. Truly, it would take adjudication to sort out the details of the reporting or not reporting based on the convoluted terminology in Reporting Requirement 210.115.1-210.115.3 RSMO. On the surface of it, though, we felt Steve should have reported Brandon's behavior, just as two others involved in this saga had already done in 2012.

From there, Steve launched into a sermon-like discussion on the victims forgiving the one who sinned against them.

---

[77] Ibid.

Most people in the room were seasoned believers who didn't need to have forgiveness defined for them, yet it was important for the pastor to establish his superior position as the teacher on the subject. He was respectfully rebuffed in short order for going off topic.

The lady who asked the question in the first place, maybe fifteen minutes earlier, simply stated her position that Steve had not answered her question about what the church was doing to help the victims. Steve moved back a little and calmed his level of frustration. Elder #5 stepped in to mention that the elders would consider her request for continued counseling. The discipleship minister mentioned access to services through his wife, who was an accredited counselor. Another attendee brought up the meeting with Dawn Varvil, asking that the facts be presented to the congregation to quell all the questions and avoid rumors. He asked for leadership transparency, though not in so many words. It turned out that a congregational meeting was exactly what leadership wanted to avoid at all costs, hence their plan to break the body into specific groups, limiting the intimidation factor.

Another audience member asked a question about the specifics of the charges and Steve's discussion with Dawn Varvil. It was apparent that he had read the case study. Steve moved to take center stage again to declare that the charges about the meeting with Dawn and the charges by the whistleblowers for not reporting Brandon and letting down the victims were false. His face grew more flushed as he stated:

> This is highly sensitive stuff, but it has been moved from the fact that somebody wants to make a charge.
> An outside person wants, a non-authorized self-investigator wants to investigate the situation, if they demand to know what happened in a private conversation between two pastors and a parent from two, from three years ago, we do not have an obligation to communicate to that self-appointed investigator what happened in that conversation. I, I hope you understand that there was, we, if there's a police investigation, that's one thing. There is a very clear line that changes if the person we talked to makes a charge against me or the previous executive minister who met with Dawn and the whistleblowers, that is a false charge. We have a legal right, an obligation to defend ourselves. To say what happened in that meeting, and to say what is being said is not true. And we can demonstrate that with evidence,

and we will do whatever it takes, um, to help that person to
withdraw that false accusation. I will say that those meetings
have been happening privately, with efforts with everybody
who's made accusations. We have had opportunities to
communicate, to respond, and try to meet with each of them
individually. I can't say that to this point we have met with
success to get them to withdraw the charges. But I will say
that in the next two weeks there will be more disclosure in
terms of the public statement, and opportunity, that we look
at, in terms of those outside the church.[78]

The topic turned quickly to the number of competent ministry leaders and
long-time members who had left the church in the past several years.
"KD," a member, who had taught Sunday school for two years, put it on
the line in many ways.

But now, the accusation has come that it is one person that is
causing this problem. And I'm not saying it is; I'm saying
that that's the accusation. And many first accounts that I
have spoken with are saying have said that. I was
wondering if, um, in order to help the situation if um, Steve,
if . . . some of the accusations have been that your
authoritarian leadership has, um, not allowed certain people
to use their God given gifts in a way that, ya know, maybe
they thought, and maybe it wasn't right, but I'm just saying
that's what I've heard over and over from people I deeply
respect, and miss that they're not ministers at our church
anymore. Um, I did not have strong personal relationships
with them, so it's not like I'm upset that they left because I
miss them greatly. But I miss their ministry and their
preaching, and their um, and the way that they helped my
children and things like that. So, I was wondering, to answer
that, um would you be willing, Steve, would you be willing
to submit to Spiritual counseling, leadership counseling and
emotional counseling? Whatever you wanna call it. Um, to a
counselor that's not related to our church, um, to maybe
answer some of those accusations from multiple people who
I know you've loved, I know that you have ministered with.
These are not people that, fly by night people, these are

---

[78]Ibid.

people that have been here, families who've been here twenty, thirty, ya know twenty years, grew up with you, that have said, "I've spoken personally with him, I did what I thought the Bible asked me to do and nothing was resolved, and I felt released and that had I to leave the church, I could no longer worship there, um, under that type of leadership," so I was just wondering would you be willing to do that?[79]

Steve looked at her and began questioning the validity of her being at the meeting. She had been teaching in his church for two years, and he didn't know who she was. He pivoted quickly to take the victim role. His technique was commendable.

Um, I will say that I have some very godly counsel, as I have gone through pain, I . . . There are three roles of our elders, oversee the congregation and see to its wellbeing, oversee their own eldership and see to its wellbeing, and the third is to oversee the senior pastor and see to its wellbeing. And in defining that I'm one set of elders, but I'm also submissive to the eldership, and there are a number of times when decisions, recent decisions where I say, I'll tell ya what I'm feeling, I'll tell ya that I'm hurting, I need you guys to pray for me, but I also need you to guide me on this decision because I'm, I'm right here. So, I think publicly the support of the elders and I have invited others to help me in the area of my personal health, um, and my own management of anxiety and stress, and I will continue to do that. And I thank you for that expressed concern for me. I can't speak for everybody that's gone. And, aah, I think our focus really needs to focus on those who we love and have stayed. I think we actually need to celebrate, aah, the longevity of those that do serve, and not to assume that everybody has left negatively, or for bad reasons, or that somebody that wants to count every exit, and that those exits are all related to my leadership.[80]

---

[79]Ibid.

[80] Ibid.

KD's method of questioning forced Steve to come out of the authoritarian tower he had built so far to look at his part in the mess. He took the opportunity to turn the crowd from revering him as the senior minister to pitying him as the victim. It was a fascinating interchange to observe. The slings and arrows from the crowd became more pointed as the questions jabbed at the sore spots in the leadership team's story. The audacity of Steve telling us that he was submissive to the elders seems ludicrous now after what I've learned while researching this project.

One of my fellow Celebrate Recovery leaders stood up and made a two-part statement. He unfolded his greater-than-six-foot frame in the row in front of me to speak with his back to me.

> But the point that I raised was the question was, what is the root cause of the problem? Brandon Milburn can happen anywhere. The fact that it's bared its ugly head again is an issue. I asked that question last week (at the teachers' meeting), Steve responded, and then I raised a question, why do we have such a mass exodus of, both congregation, volunteer staff and then as leaders for years and years. Um, and this is the difficult part, Steve said, responded, that um, people are mobile now, [the riots in] Ferguson might have been an issue, people um, there's loyalty issues, there's these types of things.
>
> Um, the next morning I received no fewer than five emails and contacts from those former ministers. Each of which indicated that they left because of leadership. Because they could not work with it, under that leadership. That was five, five people the next morning. They, these, this is the people that left. Now that's, I mean, in this certain, that's one, one, one point. The second point that I'm asking, um, and maybe this is standard operating procedure, I don't know. But Brandon came from South Eastern Christian Church in Louisville? Our counsel is from Southeast, the same church, the same church, right? Brandon's mother is employed at that same church? His family goes to that same church? Is that a conflict of interest? It seems like there are ties to that church, it just . . .[81]

---

[81] Ibid.

Steve broke in with information on SECC being a megachurch of about 28,000 members, emphasizing that SECC had volunteered the counsel. Steve stated that both churches had done a background check on Brandon. I have since made the connection between the two churches as mentor (SECC) and mentee (FCCF). I wonder how much of this inter-church counseling was getting the narrative straight between them in order to minimize damage to the churches, both of which hired Brandon. How much was damage control and face-saving? I may never know the answer to that question, but I am allowed to ask it.

An elderly woman stood to be heard. She asked whether the incidents of sexual abuse happened at the church. Steve answered her kindly, calling her "Mama L." She was obviously a longtime member. She spoke fondly of Charles Wingfield and stated that she had been at the church for twenty-five years. I bring her up here because she epitomizes the position; I found myself unable to totally understand. Without taking in the entire situation, she focused on her beloved celebrity pastor. It was a common reaction from other church members in days to come.

> I understand. So, what I can say from my heart is that we as a church, pray for our minister and pray for the staff because that, those people who need, and Steve really needs the prayer. If anybody's hurting, it's Steve. And so, we should let our hearts and prayers really go out to him and put our arms around him to give him the hug and the prayers, [AMEN] and everybody else, nobody else shouldn't matter because they're not going through what you all are. [AMEN] And you, the ones who gives the messages on Sunday that's beneficial for us, so. . .[82]

Some members of the crowd clapped at her comments, which dismissed Brandon's victims. Another member stood to get clarity regarding the mixed messages he was getting on loving the ministers who left and grieving their loss to the church while being told to "move on" and love the ones who stayed.

The tone of the meeting deepened as the topics became personal and pointed.

---

[82] Ibid.

My Celebrate Recovery friend stood again to say he had heard that White Flag Christian Church had stopped funding St. Louis Christian College, pending their firing of Professor Lay. Steve's brother was the pastor at White Flag Christian Church, so the question struck home. He now had to deflect any responsibility for the decision to cut funding from himself and FCCF. Steve framed his answer to hide the fact that his brother was putting pressure on the college on Steve's behalf.

Here is Steve's reply:

> Yes! I was informed of that after that decision was made by the eldership there. And it was stated simply that they love the college, and the mission of the college, and, but because a professor at the college is making an attack on a local pastor and damaging the bride of Christ, that they were going to cease support until, um, they wanted the college to be aware of that if they weren't aware of that.[83]

He continued in a halting manner to say how much he loved the college's mission and then spoke of the joint history that existed between FCCF and SLCC. He made a point of mentioning a couple of times that he would never "strong-arm or threaten" or otherwise influence what the college should do about Professor Lay and the case study. I noticed that Steve distanced himself from the action in implying he would never, but it was okay if his brother was the one influencing the college to silence Prof. Lay. Elder #5 broke in to tell the audience that attempts at meetings and communication via email had occurred between the whistleblowers and the elders, including Steve. He talked of moving toward reconciliation in some vague way and proceeded to inform us that Doug and Tamy Lay had been asked to step down as Sunday school teachers at FCCF. I am not sure how removing them was a conciliatory step.

A second Celebrate Recovery leader stood to speak. He was easy to spot with his dark hair and formidable size. Facing Steve, he gave his story of what brought him to FCCF in the first place and what kept him coming. He spoke of overcoming addiction. I knew his testimony. I also knew of several participants who had gone through Celebrate Recovery groups under his leadership.

---

[83] Ibid.

Some of them fell away, but many were captured by Christ and wrote new testimonies as redeemed believers. I knew that my friend knew all the excuses of participants not wanting to take responsibility for their actions. With the niceties out of the way, my friend opened up Pandora's Box with his bold statement.

> After, aah, Michael Frost left, nobody knew what was going on, and there's a whole bunch of questions, we had one great big meeting, and I got to talk to one elder, and the reason he left was because he was spending money. And aah, he was spending too much money. And, I said okay, I can take that. And then Titus and Chris left, and several elders left, and friends or whatever left, then a whole bunch of other families left at, around that same time. And, I'm [inaudible] a lot of people asking the same questions and praying, what do we do? Ya pray for your pastor and you pray for your ministers, that's all you can do right? Seems like I've been praying for six years and I keep seeing the same thing happen over and over and over again.

> You, sir, are in denial that you have a problem. Coming from an addiction I can see that. And also, having been a great liar, I can see that in you. Because from the people that I've known and people that I've built relationships with here, those that have left, I would believe them. Because there's ten and twelve and eighteen of them, and there's you. I'm not here to bash you, I love this church. I can't leave this church because of my son, because he doesn't wanna go. Because he loves this church. But we keep seeing the same thing happen over and over and you do this really good job Steve, you get this swirl going, and you talk for a long time and all of a sudden people go, "What the hell just happened?"

> As far as the accusations, again, I've been, have known Dawn Varvil for four years, used to babysit my kids for two of those years. She was in our Bible study when we were at the Clancy's house with [Elder #5], okay. I know and love these people. They don't lie. She wouldn't make this up. She went to you and she told you what she saw and thought this was a bad thing. She didn't see anything sexual, but when you see something that looks bad you tell the people in

charge, right? But, yet you say that's not what the conversation was about, she left on good terms and you have no idea why she would go upset to Doug and Tamy. And now you're gonna get rid of them too.[84]

I could see the anger and frustration in my friend's countenance from across the room. He took a breath and then Steve moved to the front of the stage to interject in an attempt at controlling the conversation.

> I hear you, Rich, I love you, I love your sisters and your brother [inaudible], and I hope that you'll work through that. Um, I don't agree with the things that you said, but I hear you [inaudible]. I didn't hear a question, but I did hear what you...[85]

Steve didn't finish his sentence, but he took the opportunity to turn the jab back at my friend without accepting anything that might be remotely true in the discussion. Steve hoped the other guy would work through that. Steve said he heard what Rich said, but was he listening to Rich's point? Was there nothing that Steve himself needed to work through? Then Rich voiced the question that would reverberate through the church halls for the coming months until it shook its very foundations.

> I guess the question is what are we gonna do? What are we gonna do? Something has to change. I mean, from my understanding and from talking to all the elders that have left you're the decision maker. The elders don't really do anything besides say yes. And those that didn't say yes were rushed out the door.[86]

The elders bristled at Rich calling the pastor out on his poor management skills, perhaps a little embarrassed at being called "yes men." Others in the audience joined the fray. I wondered for a minute if it wouldn't break out into far worse. I sat twisted in my chair, taking in as much as I could. Rich voiced what had been whispered for days. One-by-one, the elders took Steve's side.

---

[84] Ibid.

[85] Ibid.

[86] Ibid.

Their job description was to encircle and protect him, and they did just that. So, this is how the industrial-complex church operates, I thought.

Rich did not back down. He wanted to know what was going to be done not only about protecting the children of the church but also about protecting the integrity of the junior ministers and other members who had left the church. I thought the departures started with Michael Frost, but I realized they had begun before that. The elders' voices rose as they made the point that the reasons for the exodus of ministers didn't matter. People come and go, and it was time to move on. That phrase became the byword for many future discussions in small groups and from the pulpit. It was time to move on. Rich lowered his tone and asked how long the church had been talking about their mission to double and deepen. He made the point that neither would occur if the ministry kept getting cut off at the roots. His statement about elders having been taken out of the decision-making process stemmed back to the switch to the industrial-complex megachurch format.

Steve had been upstaged by the elders moving around him protectively. Rich took his seat, never getting an answer to what the church was going to do. The flare-up dampened some as a sister in Christ stood to ask a question. I marveled at her courage to take the floor after such an unsettling display. BK rephrased Rich's last query more directly. She specifically asked if the corrections suggested in "Is it Enough?" would be followed point-by-point within church procedures. Then she rolled back into why so many members had left the church over the past several years.

> I have a list here of fifty people who have left the church, who are close friends of mine. Basically, Faith Builders class that I started with here fifteen, sixteen years ago. Elder #3, (DE), Scott Seppelt, most recently who came and talked to you, Steve, and, and spoke some very hard words. And I know that they were hard for him, I know they were hard for Steve, but he thought they needed to be said. Um, we could have had another 400 people here last Sunday, but these people felt that they had to leave because there was a wound that just has not been healing here . . .
>
> I don't [know] when the date was when Titus and Chris and Michael started the big exodus. Um, I've contacted everyone one of these people and asked them, "Why did you leave?"

Two of them would not respond back to me, and one of them I suspected is for legal purposes. Um, only one of them told me that he left because he loved a different mission more. Every one of these people have said to me that they no longer have faith in Steve. I have stayed here, I've been a champion for Steve and asked people to pray for him, and to try and be reasonable and to look at his side as a, aah, leader of our church. But I also have to say that there have been many things said and many things happen over the last several years that we get through a phase, we're devastated, we see people leave, we're upset, we pray, we try and get through it. Things settle down, things calm down. Six months later it happens again. Why? We get the same answers. Six months later it happens again. We get the same answers.

Um, I just, I feel like, Steve, you've got two options at this point. One was suggested that you leave and part of me sees that for your family . . . I've cried on your mom's arms, I've cried on your daughter's arms, because I know that this is so horribly painful for them. Um, but I know on the other hand too, that, we, as a church, none of us are perfect, and we want reconciliation, we want our church to function. We want it to be effective . . .[87]

BK had hit Steve's hot button. Murmurs of wanting to replace Steve as senior minister swung a huge wrecking ball toward his dreams of heading a vast megachurch. She made the blunder of showing compassion for Steve's mother and family while asking that he leave his position. Steve, obviously threatened, stood and walked toward my side of the stage. With a glare, he proceeded to accuse BK of the very thing he was about to do. Steve's elevation was about three feet higher than the rest of us; he moved right to the edge of the stage, leaning slightly forward in a posture of power as he towered over the crowd.

I'd seen that look countless times in marital "discussions" between my ex-husband and me. I was familiar with the stance that implied: "I am bigger, stronger and more powerful than you, and you will hear me." Mental alarms sounded as I listened to the following interplay.

---

[87] Ibid.

Steve Wingfield: BK, I love you, but you brought my daughter and my mother into the conversation. If you have a question, I can try to answer that, but I have to answer whenever my family is brought into the conversation. Is there a question? Um, I love you BK, you're one of the most servant-hearted people that I know, you care about people beyond yourself, and I love you for that. Um, I love you even if you did nothing in this church. I can answer the question; I do need to respond to your comment about my mother and my daughter. But is there a question so that when you can deal that, we need to wrap up our time? Is there a question?

BK: How do we keep this pattern of these people from repeating itself in six months? There all . . . one of my comments on Facebook was, "why am I bringing this on Facebook?" My comment was if asked fifty people why they left and they all give me a different reason. People leave church, like you said different reasons—

Steve Wingfield: So, how do you change, this is your question moving forward? If that is your question, I would love to answer that. Because one of my tasks is to lead. And so, I think it important for leaders, and to suggest, not everybody will follow that leadership [inaudible]. I trust that you love my mother, and I trust that you love my daughter. My mother and my daughter were both, have expressed to me, they're my mother and they're my daughter, they'll talk to me. That they have, that they did not, they, were not comfortable with your hug. They both expressed that, because of this, they loved you, and they love you, and they want to love you. But you are attacking and loving at the same time. And it's hard, it's, that's hard. Um, because they want to love but yet they feel like you're wounding at the same time.

So I can speak for my family that my family is hurting and is wounded, and is hurting by people that they have loved for a long time but they naturally should want, I mean it's just a natural thing, they're going to want to defend me, and they're going to be hurt when you hurt them, or hurt me. You've hurt me, BK. I love you, um, you posted on my site, aah, yes, you are very good at social media. I have dealt with very little with social media, but one of your comments aah, tagged all of these people, which invites their name and all of their friends into the conversation. And that is, you were seeking their response on social media. Um, and I believe as of this evening, and the last time I checked, I don't read all of your stuff, I don't regularly go on your page but there were one hundred and forty comments. And, if we need to work out our church issues on social media, um, that would not be the leadership that I'm providing the church. If you are trying to provide that leadership, I would provide a different leadership.

The leadership does need to answer for this situation. We do have the seven elders in this room, and they can, aah, I thought we would have a shorter meeting; basically, answer questions one on one that . . . instead of a public setting. I do encourage you, BK, to consider that there is a value, yes, anybody can say anything that they want to say on social media, and I have sent you a private message, asking you to, um that I believe that you kind of waffle at times between support and wanting people to express themselves, and I think there's room for people to express themselves. Um, but I still believe, whether it's social media, or whether it is, the scripture says let no unwholesome word come out of talk, but only those things that are beneficial for building up others. And so that filter, I have posted that scripture, my wife has, um, Janet Ross has, and these are godly women that I think are handling the situation in a different way. And I think that there is a responsibility for us to filter what we put out in public. And it is the wild, wild West in social media. There aren't, there aren't any rules there.

Slander, aah, false accusations and artificial websites, threats to my family on Facebook Messenger. These things move in the area of fraud and these things move in the area of personal harassment. There is accountability for those things, it's never immediate. Um, but there's things outside ya know that I just ask for God's protection, and I have aah, again, I have been transparent with those things with leaders around me. Um, I will continue to love you, BK. You can't, you can't make me so mad I get mad at you. We've had conversations where we didn't agree on things in the past. I do not agree with um, what I believe was well intentioned decisions that you have made on social media. Um, and I have to say out loud to this group, I forgive you personally for the pain that you've brought into my life. And I will continue to love you. And I hope you will forgive me for anything that I have done that has brought pain into your life.

I did not go into ministry...I am not here now to hurt people, but to serve people. And if there's ever a time when I feel that I'm hurting the congregation, not people that are not a part of our congregation, if I believe that I am not honoring Christ, if God gives me a call to another ministry, I'll follow that call. But He's also given me a call not to leave when the church is hurting. I will not abandon the church. I love the church. Um, I hope my current staff supports me. I hope the current elders support me. I hope you'll, you will. If you're on the fence, find the place that's a little more predictable, um and then, then if, then it, then it feels okay when my daughter to accept a hug when she's not afraid that you'll hurt her the next day. And my mother as well. I love my mother, she's an awesome lady, she's an awesome servant, and —

BK: I actually said that.

Steve Wingfield: Said what?

BK: That when we hugged today, gave her a hug today.

Steve Wingfield: I have said what my mother has expressed to me in tears. And my mother's a very rock-solid woman. She sees you say something positive, then she sees you do other things negative and it's just a double message.

And that makes it really hard to know how to receive love if, if, if it's not consistent and it's not unconditional. And yes, my mother's hurting. But she's also a very strong woman, and she does not hold grudges, and we all make mistakes. I have made mistakes and I will continue to try and grow through the mistakes that I've made. I will continue, BK, I promise you, um to live and examine life and continue to grow. I ask you to forgive me if I have hurt you by the things I've said tonight.[88]

Steve pushed his "leadership, victim status and benevolence" masterfully, twisting the situation to his favor and away from the question at hand. We were eyewitnesses to the "induced conversation" method. Steve manipulated things masterfully. In rephrasing the question, he pointed to BK as the one needing to adjust, asking, "How do you change?" He used a similar pattern to what he did to Dawn Varvil. Can you see how he twisted what she said and accused her of waffling to make her question her own thoughts and statements? Did you pick out how Steve inferred BK was ungodly because she handled the situation differently than other women who posted scripture on social media? Did you notice how many times the word "love" came out of Steve's mouth in his attempt to present himself as the better person? What did he mean by his statement, "The leadership does have to answer for this situation?" What was their answer? What was their plan forward? BK, blown back by the verbal, emotional, and spiritual abuse foisted upon her,
quietly folded her paper with the fifty names on it and sat, tears streaming down her face. It was apparent that the senior minister's plea to forgive him if he hurt her smacked of insincerity. He turned the emotional knife he'd jabbed her with after his asking to be forgiven. My heart broke for BK. The display I just witnessed stunned me as it did several others in the crowd.

The executive minister called for comments from the discipleship minister who had not left for a better job elsewhere. He wondered why no one asked him why he stayed. I don't remember him getting an answer to his question that night, and the transcript of the meeting has nothing resembling an answer to his question either.

---

[88]Ibid.

He had served at the church longer than Michael, Titus, or Chris. He came to the church right out of college, similar to the others. He was gifted, bright, and scholarly, and he was also the grandson of the couple responsible for founding FCCF. That connection is likely the reason he stayed when others left.

I exited the meeting drained by what I just witnessed. I never expected to see my minister in the same mode of operation I had experienced from my ex-husband. I flashed back to one of our darkest arguments as I made the ten-minute drive home.

The next two weeks were dotted with sleepless nights and bad dreams. I never forgot the eyes of the abuser in my home. I can see them as I write this account of the meeting. I know the glare of someone who promises to love you while they tear you apart emotionally and spiritually. I know the look. I will never forget the look in Steve Wingfield's eyes, either.

Still in emotional turmoil, I sent the following note to a dear friend, also a member of FCCF on Thursday, April 9, 2015:

> I got to thinking on the way home that what we witnessed was classic emotional and spiritual abusive technique. I couldn't figure out why I got so unnerved until I realized that is what 34 years of marriage was like for me. I noticed that SW didn't go up against the stronger opponent in Rich but took it all out on Barb. I used to call it defend and attack, but I think a better description is deflect the true issue and go for the throat, leaving your opponent in a quivering heap. He thought of the most damaging and hurtful thing to say and he said it. I get madder and madder as I type this. I will not sit to hear any more of his preaching...but will be in the prayer room during the 9:30 service and then go to Bible study.

If nothing else, the meeting cemented my path forward. I could no longer sit under the teaching of Steve Wingfield. I could no longer give my tithe to support him. The meeting did one more thing: it drew the lines of conflict between those who wanted Steve to step down as senior minister and those who revered the celebrity minister and wanted to just "move on."

Both sides stated that they loved the church and wanted reconciliation and the damage to the church to be minimal, but both sides also wanted opposite outcomes that could not coexist. I was asked to be part of the steering committee of the group that wanted to restore the church by removing Steve. My acceptance kept me attending FCCF and listening to Steve's sermons throughout the peak months of the conflict.

Four days later, Elder #5 announced the legal pressure about to be exerted against the whistleblowers.

Here is the statement to the FCCF congregation, dated April 12, 2015:

> Today we have an important update on the conclusion to a court case involving a horrible crime. The case was about Brandon Milburn, a young man who abused two boys in 2009. Though the investigation revealed this did not take place in our building, we still grieve that as a college-age intern, he grossly violated the trust of our church and the families of his victims. After a year of open investigation and inviting other potential victims to come forward, the case ended with his guilty plea and a sentence of 25 years in prison. We know that people are hurting, a lot of damage done. And we want you to know that counseling is available if that is what you need. Sadly, as the sentencing date approached, individuals, who themselves had direct personal involvement with this intern, chose this highly charged moment to make the false charge that the leadership knew of the abuse and criminally failed to report it --- This is simply untrue. Though everyone has a right to express themselves, when that includes false accusations of criminal activity, it crosses the line. As leaders we responded privately and directly with those accusers. As elders we want you to know we have taken strong additional steps. We have secured an attorney, we have gone to the Florissant police and to the St. Louis County police offering full disclosure of all communications, including access to multiple witnesses that definitely disprove this false charge. As elders we stand 100% behind the integrity of our senior pastor. If you still have questions, we ask for your patience while the truth reveals itself.

For now, we ask you to join our elders expressing your support by your prayers and continued love for this church.[89]

The Petition

April 16 opened up a greater chasm in the church when news came out that Steve had filed a lawsuit against the whistleblowers, including FCCF in the petition as a plaintiff. The power play stoked the fires of the church split. It took the spotlight off the reporting versus non-reporting issue and placed it onto whether or not a church could biblically file a lawsuit. Not only that, the church also sued one of its members. Professor Lay was an active member of the church at the time he was served with the petition. As I stated earlier, Professor Lay was both a plaintiff and a defendant. An image of the first page of the suit is below.

The full document can be found at:

http:/storage.cloversites.com/firstchristianchurchofflorissant/documents/Verified Petition 15SL-CC01320 - 16 April 2015_3.pdf

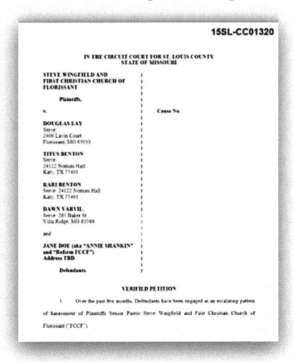

With the battle lines clearly drawn, one faction wanted to restore the church to the format prior to when the bylaws were changed. The other faction sought to remain under the ministry of Steve Wingfield. The move to include the church in the petition shaded Steve and the alleged lack of reporting issue. Instead, it became the church versus the whistleblowers' supporters. In reality, it was the senior minister and the elders using the name of the church along with potential use of church funds to protect the reputation of the senior minister and the FCCF "brand." The fifty-seven-year Wingfield dynasty at FCCF was at risk. We desired the removal of current elders and the dismissal of the senior minister in order to restore the church. We began referring to our group as "Truth and Reform FCCF." Elder #1 wrote a good summation of our position from a perspective of having been an elder during the bylaw switch.

> My view of the road to restoration goes only through the gate of removal of ineffectual or corrupt leaders (corrupt in the sense of not acting in good faith on behalf of the congregation,) installation of new elders and preaching minister, and resumption of performing our mission of reaching others for Christ and training them in the knowledge of Christ. These men have failed and need to be removed. Yes, I was one of them until March 2011, and, along with a few other deviant elders, was unable to make inroads into the leadership failures, and the promise of more to come. I believed that the elders and lead ministers at that time, of which I was one, were not ready or competent to lead us into the governance model change that was proposed by Steve W. I did agree that it would likely take some change from our original governance model to continue to grow as we desired. But, knowing our dysfunctional state of operation at the time, all I could see was SW continuing to grab power and the elders being further reduced to complete irrelevance.[90]

The other faction wanted to push it all into the memory hole and move on in order to protect the church.

---

[90] Elder #1 content posted into the Private: FCCF Truth and Reform Facebook Page, May 16, 2015. The page no longer exists. The content of the post is archived in an email sent to me via Facebook notification. Used with permission.

Steve hired a security team to ease leadership's anxiety over the dissenters. I hardly considered myself dangerous, although my stance, and that of the Truth and Reform FCCF members, that Steve should no longer be the senior minister at FCCF, was dangerous to his future. The discussions in the halls of the church building spilled into the press and all-over social media, filling threads and news feeds with the rancor within the church body. The pressure mounted and became not worth withstanding for many who simply found another place of worship. The back and forth was similar to the snippets from the leadership meeting quotes mentioned earlier.

On April 27, 2015, Professor Lay's attorney filed a fourteen-page motion for dismissal of what the lawyer called a frivolous lawsuit.[91]

Two Facebook groups were set up. "Help Restore FCCF" was a public group set up on April 28, 2015. "Truth and Reform FCCF" was a private group where church members could discuss dates and times for meetings and manage the effort administratively and strategically. A separate website housed the documents and support for the Truth and Reform FCCF group. The website also allowed access to multiple press releases that could reach further into the community. An email listing contact information for the elders allowed the members to send their questions and arguments for reform directly to the elders. We began requesting meetings before the congregation to discuss the issues transparently. We also began planning ways to speak with interested churchgoers as people went in and out, and we asked for meetings with the elders without Steve's presence.

That effort was shut down by the security team, though not before several interactions took place. The church filed orders of protection against a couple in the Truth and Reform FCCF team, along with one against Professor Lay. Police were brought into the pressure tactics to pay a visit to the couple's home. The police assessment was that nothing was out of order. Unfortunately, the order of protection meant Doug Lay could not attend the graduation ceremony of his students from St. Louis Christian College. To say that many members were incensed at the leadership's legal action is an understatement.

---

[91] See the full document here: https://isitenough.org/wp-content/uploads/2015/10/Lay_s-MTD-01874720xA1AA6.pdf.

Several were merely disgusted and found another church to attend. To say that Steve Wingfield's supporters were incensed that our group could challenge leadership and have negative things to say about the pastor is also an understatement. As I look back, it seems that we were taking part in cancel-culture warfare before it was named cancel-culture.

In an attempt to circumvent the pressure to silence the accusations against Steve and the elders, our group's steering committee wrote a letter to the church's membership, explaining the logic and defining our position. It was included in an email to FCCF members, and it ignited a fire storm of words that lit up cyberspace.

My picture, gracing an article in the local paper's June 8 "Lifestyles" section, brought questions from the curious and negative statements from the offended. Members of Steve's family wrote to me, saying that I should be ashamed of myself through emails and Facebook Messenger. Some of them also told me that in person. Their shame tactics did not change the facts as I saw them. I received emails from some friends with legitimate questions, and I answered them as honestly and forthrightly as I could. I had at least two longtime friends tell me that they loved me, but they thought I was wrong. The questions voiced in the April 8 leaders' meeting reverberated, "What is going to be done about the pastor's poor management? What about the victims? What was the church doing to help the victims?"

The Truth and Reform team kept pushing to be heard. Steve and the elders arranged for a meeting with two local pastors to mediate between the whistleblowers and Steve. Doug Lay wrote a detailed account of the crisis at FCCF.

> The crisis at FCCF was birthed out of mismanagement, deception, cover-up, and denial—by the elders of First Christian Church of Florissant, of allegations of sexual misconduct by Brandon Milburn towards 6 minors—an extremely serious situation since Brandon IS a convicted child molester of two different victims! So how have the elders dealt with the mismanagement, deception, cover-up and denial of the allegations?
>
> 1) These elders have sent the lead elder, the initiator of the mismanagement, deception, cover-up, and denial, on a six-month paid sabbatical;

2) these elders have refused to investigate the initial allegations by talking with the parent who brought the allegations to them;

3) these elders filed a lawsuit, asking for $25,000 and punitive damages against those of us who simply told them about the allegations;

4) these elders then publicly posted on the FCCF church website that they never intended to seek financial penalties although the lead elder signed his name on the lawsuit;

5) these elders dropped the lawsuit after public pressure from the press "without prejudice "- 48 hours before the lawsuit would have been dropped "with prejudice";

6) these elders have continued to ban six people from the church property;

7) these elders posted two documents on the FCCF church website with numerous falsehoods along with the dropped lawsuit;

8) these elders attended the court hearing where the temporary restraining order was denied, yet continue to post the TRO on the church's web site;

8) these elders mailed out a document in June containing multiple falsehoods that was refuted by Titus;

9) these elders have not reached out personally to the two victims and their families;

10) these elders supported the decision to provide limited free counseling by requiring victims to contact a staff member at the very church that had employed their predator, that had covered-up the allegations of their abuse, and who sued the whistle blowers of the allegations;

11) these elders supported a staff member (Virgil) who offered to take custody of Brandon if he had been released on bail;

12) these elders supported the wife of a staff member (Barb) who testified at Brandon's sentencing saying, "I want you to please believe me, if I had any doubt that Brandon would harm any young person now or in the future . . . I wouldn't be standing on this side to speak for Brandon." and "I believe he is a very different man than the kid of years ago. I think he exhibits security, not fear, patience, not impulse, and wisdom.";

13) these elders promised to answer questions asked by me, Kari Benton, and numerous other individuals but who did not keep their promises;

14) these elders supported the church dropping mission support to (a long-supported missionary and his wife, because he was part of the Restore FCCF group;

15) these elders oversee and support three staff members who are related to the lead elder who initiated the mismanagement, deception, cover-up, and denial of the original allegations of sexual misconduct by Brandon;

16) these elders, through a staff member (Dennis), are asking people, after all of this, to support their leadership, "The leaders need (I need) your grace and support. Trust is something earned so

I don't ask blinding for that, but I do ask for grace and support for men who are doing the best with what they have at this point;

The elders are like the youngest son, who after demanding his inheritance, squandering it in a distant land, and feeding pigs on a farm, ask other people (Dennis and Joe) to write to his father, asking the father to come to the distant land to help him feed pigs on the farm while asking the father to provide grace and support for the youngest son BEFORE he ever came to his senses and said, "Father, I have sinned against heaven and before you. I am no longer worthy to be called your son. Treat me as one of your hired servants.'"

I am ready to celebrate with a feast as I wait for the son to return, but I will not be making a home delivery of a fattened calf to a distant land![92]

The St. Louis Post-Dispatch reported the case dismissal that was filed on May 11 of the petition against the whistleblowers. The dismissal allowed the plaintiffs to reactivate the petition within a two-year period, holding a club over the defendants' heads.

---

[92] Douglas Lay, Facebook post July 25, 2015

The day following the dismissal, the president of SLCC ordered Professor Lay to openly thank the pastor and the elders for dropping the lawsuit and apologize. Otherwise, Lay would face disciplinary measures. The version of the SLCC contract for the following year placed a gag order on Prof. Lay, and he rebutted with his letter of resignation on May 18, the text of which is reprinted here:

> It is with great regret that I submit my resignation from my position as Professor at SLCC effectively immediately. I have enjoyed my seventeen years with SLCC, and I consider it a great honor to have been afforded the opportunity to teach and mentor future church leaders. I will always have wonderful memories of the relationships that I have had with the SLCC family.
>
> As you know the last several months have been a very difficult time for all of us in the SLCC family and have placed a great strain on relationships here as well as the school's long-term relationship with my former church FCCF. Given the status of FCCF as a major supporter of SLCC as well as the sheer number of SLCC employees who are members and leaders in the church, the recent lawsuit against me has been profoundly difficult. I can understand the conflict that it has put the school in and your desire for me to try to reach a measured reconciliation with the leadership at FCCF and move on. Unfortunately, those well-intended goals are simply impossible to accomplish as long as the current Pastor and leadership remain at FCCF. I feel I have been placed in a position where I feel compelled to continue to communicate publicly in order to (1) ensure that Brandon Milburn's victims receive the care they are entitled to; and (2) contradict the falsehoods that are being perpetrated by Steve Wingfield and the Elders of FCCF. I realize that the only way to effectively do that is to remove myself from the SLCC faculty. I am certainly sorry for any of my actions that have hurt SLCC or you personally. I think you know that it was not my intent.
>
> There will likely be those who will attribute my resignation to pressure from you. I want to emphasize that this is my own decision and done in recognition of the difficult position this whole situation places you and the institution

in. Although we have not always agreed, I appreciate what you and Dr. Chambers have done for the college. For that reason, you are free to share this letter with anyone who has any questions or concerns.

I pray for only God's best for the college and for you as you lead SLCC into the future.

In Christ,

Douglas Lay[93]

The fray continued through April and May. Prof. Lay's attorney issued a five-page press release on May 20, describing the petitions and misinformation, along with establishing that Lay reserved the right to consider his own legal options for the future. The statement included a demand for a clear and final dismissal of the lawsuit, with prejudice. It ended with a damning statement against Steve Wingfield and FCCF:

> Doug Lay and his attorney, Al W. Johnson, believe that there are many sincere and decent people at the First Christian Church of Florissant. Unfortunately, Pastor Steve Wingfield and the current leadership of the Church have failed in their leadership duties to their members as well as to the victims of Mr. Milburn's horrific crimes.[94]

The topic for Wingfield's May 31 sermon[95] was part of a series called "Path to Restoration." This one had to do with sibling rivalries. I paraphrase, "How do we keep from allowing sin and division from coming in the door? How can we recognize it and address it before it does damage? We let it in to our own lives, not realizing that sin will divide and bring disunity. We can't control what everybody else does, right? But we can control what we let into our own lives. We can guard the door of our own church family, of our own marriage, and of our own relationships with our kids, and we say anger, jealousy, and competition and hate—I'm not letting it in my door.

---

[93] https://restorefccf.org/professor-lay-resigns-from-st-louis-christian-college/

[94] https://restorefccf.org/professor-lays-press-release-5-18-2015/

[95] https://vimeo.com/129790372

I will not let it master me. I'm going to love. I'm going to be my brother's keeper."

This paraphrase of the sermon, taken out of context of the greater picture, seems innocuous enough. However, one glaring point is left out, and I noticed it as I watched the sermon on Vimeo. Steve is the biblical shepherd of a flock of believers. It is his responsibility to protect his flock. In the sermon, he inferred that the dissenters who received orders of protection were the "sin" that he and the elders were keeping from the doors of the church. I found it ironic that he was about ten years too late in keeping the sin from the flock. He allowed Brandon through the gate to begin with, which was reasonable, because Brandon passed the scrutiny of a security check at the time. On the other hand, once Steve got the information from the three informants, Steve allowed the threat to the church back through the doors multiple times. Brandon was even allowed to lead VBS. Steve not only let Brandon to enter the FCCF facility, he also sent him to other churches, along with a personal recommendation. This is unconscionable. Steve began the story in the middle, where he could avoid culpability for letting the wolf into the pen repeatedly.

Sermon topics tried to soothe the open wounds amongst the congregation while castigating the Truth and Reform FCCF folks. Some church members took it upon themselves to seek unity by encouraging prayer on behalf of the church. One of my friends requested a prayer meeting time slot from the executive minister and was given the go ahead to have her prayer gathering on May 31. She asked me to prepare a section of it, and I accepted the opportunity. The executive minister permitted us to use the sanctuary for the meeting but neglected to clear it with Steve. We prayed through the ACTS of prayer: Adoration, Confession, Thanksgiving, and Supplication.

I stood before those who accepted the invitation to the meeting to give my part of the presentation in full view of Steve. Anger narrowed his eyes and twisted his face. It was my turn to stand on the stage overlooking his seat to pray for the church that he wanted to dominate. The abuser's eyes showed no appreciation for the prayers or what they represented to the people in the pews.

June 4 marked the date of Dawn Varvil's demand letter from her attorney to Steve's attorney. (I have mentioned the details of her demands under her introduction as a main character.) As a parent of one of the youth group members whom Brandon helped lead, her son had been exposed. She had every right to set forth her structure for helping the victims. That was her main impetus.

Steve's sermons from the pulpit centered on the path to restoration. His June 7 topic incorporated several verses that encapsulated the need for restraint. He spoke of the restraints of government and the God-given restraints of conscience, family, civil authority, and the church. He likened the church to "salt to preserve what would otherwise decay in our society." He went on, "So when we go through times of brokenness, it is important to reinforce and strengthen and lean into the church, the structure that God has supplied. How do we do that? How do we support the church, because the church is always imperfect, yet beautiful, God-ordained? First, we have to fight for it, not against it. Support the leaders. Pray. Instead of being a critic, find something positive. Increase of giving over previous years."[96] At that point he dropped the all-too-frequent call for money.

As I watched this message, I was struck by the lack of duty and conscience in Steve's talk. What about the restraint of a duty to report alleged abuse? Where was Steve's conscience when he gave Brandon job recommendations after he had been made aware of Brandon's alleged misconduct? Where was Steve's accountability?

I posted the following prayer on my Facebook page on June 8, 2015.

> Father and Almighty God, who is above all. You set our universe and the galaxies into motion and ignited the stars, especially the one that warms our planet and grows our food. There is no one with your righteousness and no one with your great power. I come humbly to the base of your mercy seat this morning with an uplifted heart, but a heavy burden for my church body. I thank you for every one of my brothers and sisters in Christ. I thank you for those who are bold to confront evil. I thank you for those who stand ready for action on your behalf. I thank you for those who stand in

---

[96] https://vimeo.com/130445197

prayer for righteousness, truth and justice. I thank you for your stand on those topics, too. I read in your Word that you will not be mocked. What a man sews, so shall he also reap. Your recompense is sure and swift. Your reward will not be given those who falsely teach and lead your flock astray. You will not reward those who live in idolatry, seeking fame and numbers and church size. No, You will not be mocked. Your wave of justice will crash. I may not see it in my days, Lord, but I know it is sure. One day, there will be an accounting for those who will not be held accountable in this life. One day, they will stand before a Holy and just God to give a full accounting. Your will be done, Father. Help us take the steps to complete our due diligence. Make Your way known to us as we wend our path through these dark days. Be our light. Be our strength. I thank You that You are who You say You are, and that You will do what You say You will do. I pray in the name and authority of Jesus, according to Your good and perfect will, Amen.

The FCCF elders mounted a further strike against one of the Truth and Reform FCCF leaders and his wife, banning them from the premises of FCCF as of June 13, 2015. It's fascinating how efforts to intimidate and silence tend to solidify the dissidents' positions and increase their message. I would have thought the elders might know how that works from the perfect example of persecution of the apostles. The Truth and Reform FCCF members emailed their case to the membership. Below is a copy of their letter.

The Elders of First Christian Church of Florissant:

"Help Restore FCCF" was born of a concern held by many members that FCCF has strayed far from its primary purpose which is simply stated in ARTICLE II of the By-Laws: "The purpose of the congregation shall be to fulfill the great commission of Jesus Christ as expressed in the New Testament, particularly as stated in Matthew 28:18–20."

It is in support of this stated purpose, nothing more and nothing less, that we felt compelled to write this letter at this time.

It has become apparent that FCCF has developed major faults in the integrity of the church body — faults that continue to widen daily. We understand that failure to return to our founding purpose will inevitably lead to the collapse of the church we love. The church body is — and has been — in a poor state of health for quite some time. Many know this, many suspect this, and still others remain blind. The reemergence of the Milburn case was simply the flashpoint that moved many of us to act.

Though certainly the most publicized and disconcerting issue the church has faced, the crimes perpetrated by Milburn must not be viewed in isolation, but rather as one more consequence of a consistent pattern of an inadequate, unhealthy and abusive leadership. The manner in which the turmoil surrounding the initial Milburn revelations was addressed, and the manner in which the aftermath of those events has been allowed to fester in the subsequent months, speaks conclusively to the flawed and fundamentally ineffective leadership guiding the congregation.

As painful as it might be, we must ask some direct, specific and difficult questions:

- Has Steve Wingfield faithfully carried out the task of shepherd, overseer, and pastor?
- Has he demonstrated that he can be relied upon to lead our congregation selflessly, without an eye on personal aspirations, as he seeks to grow the body of Christ in Florissant?
- Is his primary focus fulfillment of the Great Commission of Jesus Christ?

Furthermore, we must also ask:
- Have the elders fulfilled their role to support, counsel, and advise the Senior Pastor, to enable him to fulfill his role and further the stated purpose of FCCF?
- Have they provided support and counsel to the congregation in their efforts toward that objective, as well?

We believe that a review of the actions taken and decisions made by FCCF leadership must be examined thoroughly and objectively: doing so leads to one undeniable conclusion.

Failings in Leadership and the Overall Decline of FCCF During the past seven years our church has experienced an alarmingly high staff turnover, an equally alarming decline in attendance, and unwise stewardship of church funds.

1. In 2010, Steve began to lead the elders through by-law changes to shift management of the church from the elders to the paid staff, with himself as the senior decision maker. This was to provide a framework to allow for greater church growth. In 2012, with little to no explanation and justification to the congregation, Steve and the elders proposed and secured a change in the church by-laws. The change resulted in a tightening of Steve's personal control over the eldership and all decision-making in the church.
2. Since Steve Wingfield became Lead Pastor, thirteen key ministry staff members have left the church; seven in the past 18 months. When asked why they left, most cited Steve's leadership style and the inability to establish a working relationship with him as the primary reasons, if not the only reason, for departure.
3. [Elder #5], the Chairman of the Elders and Congregation, recently resigned as the chair, yet the congregation has not been formally advised as of today. It was learned on June 7th that he had also resigned as an elder, between the 8:00 and 9:30 services that morning. In response to questioning FCCF eldership on whether [Elder #5] resigned, the eldership response was "this is a personal matter." The reason for [Elder #5's] resignation may be a personal matter; however, his resignation is a church matter.
4. Steve has claimed that he has been threatened by individuals. When one of his own security guards asked for evidence of such threats, Steve was unable

to produce anything. The security guard resigned soon afterward.

5. Attendance at our church has declined, even as we continue to baptize new believers and add new members.

6. More than a hundred long-time and influential individuals have left the church (documentation available). As a result, many ministry areas have weakened due to lack and experience of volunteers.

7. The church sold the Kirk House, a useful venue for counseling and a successful community outreach ministry, for $84,900. That was approximately the same amount spent to hire a consultant for strategies to increase giving, which resulted in the "I'm All In" campaign. Six months later, the congregation has not been apprised of the results of   this campaign.

8. The recent offerings trend indicates the church may be about to face a general decline in income, to be compounded by the typical decline in attendance and giving in the summer months.

9. Many have been confused by the conflict they have witnessed in recent months: the name calling, the accusations, shouting from the mouths of alleged Godly men. Months have passed where the elders have exhorted us to reach out to them, to call them, to email them, affirming that they are here to help, willing to provide answers when possible. Unfortunately, the collective summary of those who have made such attempts, including unanswered emails and voicemails, and the now all too familiar, "We'll get back with you on that," characterizes a pattern of hurt and frustration. If dialogue is engaged, legitimate questions are treated as accusations, and the accuser becomes the adversary — an example of spiritual abuse. If one questions, disagrees, or doubts, that person becomes the enemy — an example of bullying.

Mishandling of Sexual Misconduct Allegations

Church leadership, largely revolving around Steve Wingfield, has demonstrated a failure to take actions to care for those impacted by Brandon Milburn and to ensure no other children suffer such abuse.

1. Scott Seppelt (in 2011) and Dawn Varvil (in 2012) brought to Steve their concerns about Brandon Milburn's inappropriate and alarming misconduct with children. These concerns were not reported or investigated, and Brandon was permitted to continue to have access and contact with FCCF youth.
2. Steve has maintained in at least two "public announcements" from the pulpit that neither he nor the church has "ever" been made aware of concerns regarding Brandon Milburn or "any" reports of disturbing activity between Brandon and any minor. The then Chairman of the Elders, [Elder #5], made a third similar statement, at a later date, in all three worship services. Steve and the elders, however, have yet to make a single retraction of this position.
3. The statement released to the press by FCCF on February 11, 2014 stated, "For the last several years he (Brandon) has been living in another state." Brandon, however, had been living in St. Louis, working at an area church, attending Sunday night services at FCCF, and leading at the church's Vacation Bible School — all during the time the church had reported Brandon living in another state. Steve Wingfield or the elders have never provided an adequate explanation for this discrepancy.
4. Church leadership has never contacted the family of one of the victims, nor has church leadership sought out to identify, care and support any other victims.

Conclusion and Recommendation

We take no pleasure in revealing this summation of Steve Wingfield's failure in the capacity of Senior Minister, or the elders' failure to provide Steve counsel and the congregation guidance in this time of turmoil.

But to obey 1 Timothy 5:20, the truth must be brought to light. Steve requires Biblical discipline. We must follow the guidance of 2 Timothy 3:16, using Scripture to lovingly rebuke and correct Steve.

Our church needs to go through a difficult time of healing. Steve has harmed many people, has denied any wrongdoing, and offers no repentance. To think he could lead the healing process for the very people he has hurt is inconceivable.

But what must be done to accomplish the restoration and reconciliation we all want for our church? We prayerfully submit the only possible way to even begin the process is with either the resignation or removal of Steve Wingfield as Lead Pastor. Should the elders fail to act on or provide reasonable response to this request, there would be no option but to interpret that failure to act or respond as a tacit rejection of our requests, at which point we would be compelled to escalate the requests to the status of "demands." These demands would in turn be applicable to the elders as well as Steve. Your failure to assist in the resolution of this situation would be in direct conflict with your role of representation, propagation, and protection of the faith and interests of the congregation.

This congregation is and shall always remain autonomous in government, recognizing Christ as its sole head" (FCCF By-Laws, 2012). The support for this position is in evidence by the signatures provided in following:

We, the undersigned, have read and reviewed pages 1–4 of this letter. We thereby offer our signatures in support of Steve Wingfield's immediate resignation or removal from First Christian Church of Florissant.

Guest preachers filled the pulpit to present additional portions of the "Path to Restoration" series. The next two weeks brought megachurch pastors from outside the church. The first one spoke about a torn life and the message that "He's given you good and godly leaders and now is the time to rally together in the spirit of Christ around the leaders that God has placed here to move this thing forward and get after the mission that God's given you." In other words, those of us in the pews were to move on.

Point and counterpoint went on between the two factions of the church. The church elders released a letter dated June 21, 2015, to church members to which Titus Benton posted his comments line-by-line in rebuttal. The statements in <u>plain text</u> are by the elders. The **bolded statements** are those of Titus Benton. I received a paper copy of the letter on FCCF letterhead. Electronic versions were also distributed. We did not move on; we pressed on.

> Dear Brothers and Sisters in Christ,
>
> We're blessed. First Christian Church of Florissant is an amazing multi-generational, multiethnic family. We joyfully celebrate a 57-year legacy of ministry built on honoring Jesus Christ through compassionately living in the world . . .
>
> **This is true. For fifty years, there were few better examples of Great Commission churches in the United States. So, moving was this history that I wrote my master's thesis on the rich history. It is one worthy of great honor.**
>
> We have served thousands of families and been recognized nationally for the strength of our diversity. Like every family, our church family has moments when our strength is tested. This is one of those moments. In January 2014 two former First Christian Church families were told for the first time by their now grown sons that they had been sexually abused in 2007 by Brandon Milburn. . .
>
> **Two questions:**
>
> **1. How do the elders know those families were told in January? They have talked to one of the families**

sparingly and the other not at all. I know this because I spoke with the families.

2. **The victims were not abused in 2007 alone, but from2007 – 2009. To continue to cite this date inaccurately seems to victims to be a minimization of what occurred to them in order to save face.**

. . .then a full-time student at St. Louis Christian College and a part-time church employee. These families did the right thing, the difficult thing. They stood strong in their test . . .

They are strong, but I would not say they stood strong. They were crumpled to the floor in agony. They wept. They were broken. They hurt. And again, I'm not sure how the elders would know that they stood strong "in their test," because there was little to no communication between the families and the church.

. . .reported this horrible crime to the authorities and sought counseling. A year-long open investigation invited any other victims to come forward and led to a guilty plea and a sentence to 25 years in prison . . .

The investigation by law enforcement did not last a year. And there was no investigation by church leaders (unless a handful of announcements counts as an investigation). At first, there was a not-guilty plea and the defendant minimized his actions. At the last second, when facing trial, Brandon changed his plea to avoid a trial.

While this abuse did not occur in church facilities or at our programs, we hurt when others do. . .

There is no doubt in my mind church leaders hurt to learn of Brandon's betrayal of trust and predatory behavior. I believe that is true. However, this is not the abuse that Steve was confronted about or what the recent controversy is surrounding. For the better part of the last four months, private conversations with Steve and elders made this clear. The recent confrontation was regarding abuses in addition to the charges against Brandon, and warnings of that abuse that were shared with Steve in 2011 and 2012.

The actions of one had a ripple effect of hurt to many through his violation of trust. Because we are a place of healing, First Christian provides two professional counseling resources available for victims of Milburn's abuse.

There's a lot to be said here. First, many were hurt by his violation of trust. But, again, that's not what the recent confrontation has been about. It has been about hurt caused by the elders' (including Steve) and the violation of the trust placed in them, beginning with (but not limited to) their inactivity when approached about additional abuse concerns shared with Steve in 2011 and again in 2012. This abuse was not related to the charges against Brandon but was inflicted upon additional victims. There is no mention of this in this open letter, and that is deceitful. No one was ever claiming that Steve (or anyone, for that matter) knew about abuse in 2007 – 2009. However, most readers of this Open Letter surely read recent news stories of first-hand accounts from additional victims claiming that they were abused by Brandon in 2011/2012. Additionally, while First Christian did offer counseling, the elders started this document by granting that the known victims and their families were no longer involved at First Christian. So, the counseling they reportedly "offered" was not known by those families, because those families were not in services to hear the announcement — the only place those services were spoken of.

Disturbing methods. Since the February 2015 sentencing . . .

Brandon Milburn's sentencing was in late March, not February.

First Christian Church has been harassed and slandered by false claims that church leaders knew of the sexual abuse and criminally failed to report it. This is simply not true . . .

Actually, it is true. In 2011 and again in 2012, two different individuals told Steve Wingfield of concerns regarding behaviors indicative of abuse. I am the only one to allege this was a crime, which I shared with Steve and the elders

privately on one occasion. This was after hearing about the concerns first-hand and doing my own investigation to ensure that they were true before confronting them. I came to the elders and Steve through a private letter that alerted them to that which I had been made aware. Even though I was the only one to allege that it is a crime, it is worth noting that failure to report suspected child abuse (not proven child abuse, but suspected) is a crime. It is also only fair to admit that it was later included in the case study and received a much wider audience.

"Harassment" and "slander" are two legal terms used to describe a criminal offense that the cited behavior does not rise to the level of. The restraining order that asserted that these behaviors were present was ruled against in the court of law, so to still describe the behavior "against" the church as harassment and slander is legally untrue and as an adjective in a piece of communication like this is a poor choice as it does not represent the truth.

These unsubstantiated claims . . .

The claims were not unsubstantiated. They were verified by several people before I ever contacted church leadership.

. . .were repeatedly promoted in the unfiltered platform of social media . . .

Sort of like the elders' open letter that I'm now commenting on.

. . .on fake Facebook accounts, in phone calls and emails sourced through the unauthorized use of church databases, in issuing demands for the resignation of leaders and seeking supporters who might disrupt worship services . . .

to this day, the elders have offered no evidence of harassing phone calls or e-mails, nor that there were those who had the goal of disrupting worship services.

. . .Critics do share a valuable role suggesting need for improvements. However, some opportunistically choose destructive methods. . .testing great cities, testing law enforcement, testing best of class organizations, schools, and even effective churches . . .

To assert that someone was being opportunistic infers that they are seeking selfish gain. Though church leaders have hinted at hidden agendas on the part of whistleblowers, they have never indicated what these agendas might be. As for the various institutions that have been tested, only First Christian has faced critique and ridicule. And outside of the crimes of Brandon Milburn (and the mishandling of concerns on the part of church leadership in the wake of his arrest), it is easy to argue that FCCF has not been "effective" in various ministry pursuits in recent years. In other words, the people watching all this and yelling "fire" are not the ones that lit the match. There are bigger problems at FCCF than Brandon Milburn.

A line must be drawn. These methods do not belong in our church family.

Patient leadership. As elders, we have worked in unity over the last months to protect and clear First Christians name legally and through law enforcement . . .

Understand this phrase "a line must be drawn." They are drawing it. If you do not agree with church leaders, you do not belong in our church family. It has been assumed throughout this that protecting First Christian's name was the leadership's goal based on how these issues have been handled. While some churches would've preferred to seek the truth, minister to victims, and correct mistakes, their goal—now stated clearly for all to see and understand—was to clear their name and protect their reputation.

Based on the clear evidence, we've sought retractions, not financial penalties . . .

Several lawyers have read the lawsuit filed against five defendants in Saint Louis County Court—four lawyers

representing the defense and at least one additional lawyer giving advice. Each of them have been clear—financial penalties of at least $25,000 were being sought in the lawsuit against the defendants, and Steve Wingfield's signature was on the page following that request. To assert that retractions and not financial penalties were what was being sought is, simply put, not true.

After pursuing options that enabled us to name accusers and present affidavits and evidence that could be substantiated in court . . .

The elders do not note here that it could NOT be substantiated in court. . .the restraining order that named the accusers and attached the affidavits and provided the evidence was denied by a court in Saint Louis County.

. . .the eldership decided to voluntarily drop civil actions and enlist assistance from two respected Christian mediators . . .

This is not true. My wife and I were in the meeting where the elders were asked to drop the lawsuit—by the "mediators" that had sought the elders and the Bentons out. How is (it) that the elders can now claim to have voluntarily dropped the lawsuit in order to instead enlist assistance from outside mediators when the mediators were brought in first and ended up being the ones who asked them to drop the suit?

. . .Our intent—to give our critics yet additional opportunities to reconcile. Regretfully, those seeking to blame us and incite outrage prefer to continue spreading wholly false accusations.

Following the dropping of the lawsuit, only my wife and I were reached out to for further dialogue. This dialogue happened on one occasion and did not include any talk of reconciliation, only a rehashing of past events and arguments as to why they had to be that way. In fact, after forty minutes of this banter, the "mediator" decided he'd heard enough and excused himself to go home. Additionally, as it has already been pointed out, the

accusations were not "wholly false." In fact, in the same meeting where it was requested that the lawsuit be dropped, Steve Wingfield admitted that Dawn Varvil had shared with him in the 2012 meeting that Brandon had bought an iPhone for a young man, been seen spooning with him, and had a key to his apartment.

. . .Standing strong. Upon the counsel of our mediator, we are persuaded that the best course of action for the First Christian family NOW is to refocus our energies exclusively on moving forward with our ministry and mission.

This is true. The "mediators" did not actually mediate — trying to bring two sides together. Rather, they advised church leaders to make a statement and move on. This statement is the statement following that counsel, and they sincerely have no intention of talking about this anymore.

. . .With your support and encouragement, First Christian Church will only intensify our commitment to stand strong, becoming an even more compassionate community resource. We're thankful that this amazing family continues to grow in faith, welcoming first-time guests and each week celebrating new committed followers of Christ. We began June with more than 500 kids and volunteers in Vacation Bible School. Our Celebrate Recovery is an ongoing ministry of support. While we will always have a tear in our eye for those wronged by heinous actions . . .

Since Brandon's arrest, no elder has reportedly had a tear in their eye for any victim. Only after a huge public outcry, several newspaper articles, and a drastic reduction in weekly attendance and giving did the church even arrange for counseling for victims — and those details are yet to have been shared with a wide audience.

. . .our focus is and will be resolutely on the greater things that bring us together . . . one faith, in one Lord, and one message of God's love and grace that can bring healing in any life. Better not bitter. First Christian Church of Florissant is listening, learning and loving, determined to be better, not bitter . . .

In the often-scoffed-at case study entitled "Is it Enough?" the authors provide more than a dozen suggestions at how First Christian could do better at recognizing, reporting, and handling sexual abuse within its family. As of the writing of this response, zero have been implemented. (See appendix.)

. . .Our core values determine that we will go forward, empowered by God's grace to be a place where Christ comes first, where the lost are found, where the Word is heard, where care is shared, and where our world is changed. In this time of testing, First Christian is standing strong . . .

Given the turnover in staff, decline in attendance, public outrage, divided congregation, and reported spiritual and physical unhealth of the senior pastor in the face of conflict, it is difficult to believe this assertion.

We invite you to stand with us.

The attorney for Steve Wingfield and the church responded by mail on June 26 to Dawn Varvil's letter from June 4 with a roundabout address of her demands. They wrote of their intent to increase the security for the children and to do something for the victims through an arrangement with Agape Counseling.

My clients appreciate the suggestions you made to further improve the church's response to the Milburn incident and to improve its policies moving forward. First Christian is giving those suggestions due consideration and is, of course, open to any other suggestions from your client or the community.

The church currently has no intention to reinstitute any litigation. Instead, First Christian is resolved to focus its energy on its mission as a ministry moving forward.[97]

---

[97] https://restorefccf.org/response-to-dawn-varvils-demand-letter-6-26-15/

The gist of their communication was their intent to move on, to focus on other things.

The July 7 sermon brought a second outside megachurch pastor to speak on the path to restoration, "Restoring an Image." The pew folks got a lesson on church unity, being angry but not sinning in our anger. The sermon boiled down to a cheerleading session for Steve. So, now we had the argument from authority figures to move on. We were reminded of the "elements we have to put behind us" but to speak the truth in love.

Steve returned from a megachurch pastors' conference, and he titled the last sermon in the series "Restored Strength."
During the sermon he spoke about Gideon. I suppose he was getting at the congregants disappearing from the pews. What had been a church of around 2,000 active members was quickly dwindling. He told of seventeen couples encircling him and praying for him and Beth at the Mega-church Conference, Bonita Springs, Florida, February 16-19, 2015. He spoke of seeing a rainbow when he got home as a sign of God's promise. I wondered if Steve wasn't confusing the promise not to drown Earth's inhabitants ever again with some kind of anointing on him.

On July 22, the elders informed Steve of their decision to give him a six-month sabbatical for counseling and restoration away from the church. The sabbatical was made public on July 26. We rejoiced to hear that Steve was going to be out of the pulpit and hoped that, like the majority of other pastors put on sabbatical leave, he would never return. It was a small sense of victory; however, it was marred by Elder #9's statement that, "It is important for you to know that this action is in NO way a reflection of a change of direction on the part of the elders regarding our support, trust and belief that Steve Wingfield is a man called of God to be and to serve as senior pastor here at First Christian Church."[98]

According to Elder #9's statement, the purpose of the elder-directed time away from the church was for Steve to get counseling not only for stress, grief, and emotional trauma but also to receive counseling in regard to his management style. It sounded like the elders had put Steve on the victim pedestal without one word about the true victims.

---

[98] https://restorefccf.org/elder-statement-7-26-15-to-the-congregation/

My personal opinion is that Steve was victimized by his own self-protective tendencies. He bore sole responsibility for his own destruction. However, Brandon Milburn's victims are not responsible for being targeted, groomed, and abused by a pedophile. There is no comparing the two.

The Truth and Reform FCCF members began gathering in the sanctuary of a nearby church on Saturday evenings. We established Everyday Fellowship, where we could worship and get sound scriptural teaching. We called Doug Lay to be our pastor and filed the requisite paperwork to become a 501C3 charity in good standing.

We sat on the sidelines, praying for our brothers and sisters who decided to stay with FCCF while the family life minister, the discipleship minister, and the three or four remaining elders moved on. Some members of our group began attending there in Steve's absence in prayerful hope that the changes we desired for the church would eventually materialize, should the elders permanently remove Steve. The rest of us were past going back to FCCF. After I completed the last meeting of the Celebrate Recovery twelve-step class I was leading, I never went back. It was all I could do to walk into the building for that last class. There was a darkness about FCCF that I could not shake.

The six months went by in a split-attention sort of way as Everyday Fellowship continued to grow closer as a church family. The membership dwindled as several people found larger, well-established churches to attend. The smaller the congregation became, the tighter the bonds between us grew. The announcement that Steve would be returning as senior minister came in January. Those who had gone back to FCCF to help with a possible restoration returned to the Everyday Fellowship fold, recognizing that FCCF would go back under Steve's leadership.

At the end of January 2016, the elders announced the return of the beloved celebrity pastor. In a way, they played the victim card in the post to the church's Facebook page. The church administration, as they had said many times during the height of the fray, was moving on. They mentioned the need for higher giving due to the drop in giving the previous year, but they said nothing about the true victims or how the church intended to support them.

Their announcement of the plan for Steve to return to the pulpit appeared on Facebook on February 7, 2016.

As many of you know our church has just come through a very challenging 2015, but we are looking forward to a better year as we have turned the page to 2016. It has been announced that, with the help of some special over and above offerings, we were able to make our principle and interest payments as scheduled. We are thankful to God for that. We are also excited to announce that our Senior Pastor, Steve Wingfield, will be returning from his 6-month sabbatical on January 31. He and Beth will be worshiping with us on that day and he will resume preaching on either February 7 or 14. Steve and Beth have been through a very difficult 2015, and I know they have missed their church and their church family as they have been away. We encourage each one of you to reach out and welcome them back. There are cards in the foyer that you can fill out with a greeting, share some of the ways their ministry has blessed you over the past 28 years, or a simple "welcome back" would be a blessing to them. The card can be dropped in the basket, mailed with a pre-addressed envelope, also available, or given to them in person this Sunday. We would also like to extend a thank you to our entire church staff. They have, like all of us, endured a very difficult year as well. During Steve's absence they have all stepped up in many ways to serve the church. We thank each of them for that. We also want to thank each person in this congregation for your prayers, words of encouragement, and patience as we know this time has been a challenge to many of you as well. Finally, looking forward into 2016, we have experienced a sharp decline in giving which has led to some very difficult budget challenges which will necessitate a reduction in ministry spending and staffing. We will be gathering a group of individuals from experienced pastors to those gifted in the area of finance to assemble a leadership team that will help us determine the best way to move forward for the health of our church. What can you do? While we have some very difficult decisions, practical and emotional to make, we are also looking forward to getting back to our vision to REACH, WIN, GROW. We have a great church, a great facility and a great community to serve. Most importantly, we have a great God. Please continue prayer support as we commit to getting back to the joy of serving

God with a fellowship of believers that love and support each other in all we do.[99]

The ministers, who carried the church through the difficult months of the sabbatical, received notification that their time with the church would end on February 19, 2016.
Virgil Brazzle, Dennis Hounshell, and Bob Farmer became victims in their own right of the industrial-complex celebrity minister and his crew of elders. They were notified that their contractual arrangements with FCCF would not be renewed due to the current financial difficulties that the church faced. When the ivory tower of the celebrity minister fell, it crushed the lives of those who held the fort while he was gone. When he returned, there was no longer any room for them at the inn.

Steve's returning sermon focused on the God of second chances. Ironically, we were forced to stand by our convictions, and Everyday Fellowship gave us a second chance at building a true and lasting church family, no matter how small. The ministers who were let go fought through their anger and grief over how they were treated but made second chances for themselves. Even the discipleship minister made his way through a doctoral degree in another state. They moved on, but I doubt they buried it all by the wayside. My guess is they still bear the scars of what happened at FCCF as much as we in the pews do.

The effect on church leadership further decimated the elders. In an email dated August 18, 2021, Elder #1 gave me these afterthoughts of the experience.

> This is what I mean: When the Milburn cover-up became known, there were, I believe, 7 elders, including SW, [Elder #9], [Elder #4], [Elder #6],[Elder #7], [Elder #5], and [the soon-to-be executive minister].The Sunday that the elders set for a Q&A in the lobby between services, [Elder #5] was an elder during the Q&A following the 8am Chapel service, but had resigned before the Q&A between the later services. As you witnessed, the elders were "in our faces" during the Small Group Leaders session, defending SW and berating the members of the congregation who spoke up with honest and important questions.

---

[99] https://drive.google.com/drive/folders/1iQWMl5bdomDvJhiZ8-1gV3hyTBBppMQq

Skip to the next "annual" congregational meeting where elders and deacons were to be confirmed (maybe December of 2015. . .? I don't remember being around for the election, so maybe it was spring of 2016.) Of those 7 elders, only (SW=Steve Wingfield), [Elder #6] & [Elder #4] remained. The others either resigned, were fired [the Executive Minister], or chose not to renew their position. [Elder #4] had planned to step down, but stayed, fearing there would be no one who could take on the financial mantle. So, 4 elders out of 6 left their posts (SW was elder by position). I've always wondered what precipitated this exodus since there was unwavering support earlier in the episode. Apparently, even SW couldn't hold their allegiance, or he actively sought to rid himself of them. As disheartening as this element is, I'm guessing not a handful in the congregation were really aware of this collapse in leadership.[100]

These experiences make us what we are, and God makes them glorify him, if we let him. We of Truth and Reform FCCF may have gone away from the corporate FCCF body, but we never moved away from the victims' plight. We were undoubtedly hurt by the actions of the church leadership. One member of the group summed it up as follows:

1. The "victimizer" is now being portrayed as the victim. During this time away from the church, Steve will be seeking counsel, not only to address the stress, grief, fatigue and emotional trauma that he has sustained . . . but also to address issues that have become deficits to his management and leadership style."
   a. Let's not forget the nine families that have had to uproot their households to get out from under the "leadership style" that the senior pastor uses. Titus Benton, [BB], [CN], [BP], [KG], [TB], [RG], and now [LB]—all have families that have been impacted. Granted, one or two of these families would probably have left no matter what, but, from what they have told church members, most of these families left because of the "leadership."

---

[100] Email from Elder #1 reprinted with permission.

b. Six members of the congregation are still banned from First Christian Church.
c. The sexual abuse victims have not all received care but have been offered "assistance" with questionable strings attached.
d. The defamation lawsuit is still active and can be re-filed at will within the next 20 months. The five defendants must maintain legal counsel until the lawsuit is withdrawn "with prejudice." So far, the defendants have endured over $12,000 in legal fees to protect themselves from First Christian Church's lawsuit. Doug Lay resigned from St. Louis Christian College to keep from being silenced about the sexual abuse issues.
e. Leaders at First Christian (presumably the Senior Pastor, based on comments from detectives) told enough lies to the Florissant Police Department that two detectives paid a visit to a church member's home. During that "visit" they accused the family of making email and phone threats, stealing church property (email database) and intimidating other church members on church property. The family was concerned enough that they retained legal counsel and under Missouri's "sunshine laws," found that the Florissant Police felt there was no merit to the complaints from First Christian Church. The Police Department handed over copies of the paperwork and stated that the case was closed. To date, that family is still banned from church property.

2. Church performance was ignored. Instead, a plea stating, "Perhaps, more than ever, now your contributions in the area of serving and giving are needed the most. We also need your continued prayers and trust as we still face attacks and criticisms" was issued.
a. Worship attendance has been dropping since 2007. It is down now and has been declining since Steve Wingfield was named senior pastor.
b. Overall church income is down.
c. Overall volunteerism is down.

These conditions are not the results of "attacks" and "criticisms". They are the result of a church disintegrating from the inside out.

When a church loses over half of its elders in a three-year period and 50% of its staff leaves in a two-year period, the problem isn't criticism—it is leadership. Five years ago, there were 13 elders, now there are four (discounting the senior pastor and executive pastor.)

So . . . the question becomes, who are the victims?

Is it the senior pastor dealing with the blow back from his past actions?

Or is it the staff members and their families who had to move their households to take other positions and get out from under "leadership?"

Or, is it the existing church membership who haven't been aware of the tyrant walking among them and don't understand why the church is shrinking?

Or, is it the loyal, long-term members who are standing on the street and moving to other churches because of issues with how First Christian Church has conducted itself over the last five years?[101]

What did the church do for the victims? I am back to the question that resounded at the June 8 leaders' meeting. The church leadership arranged for limited counseling for victims, with the caveat that the first visit had to be with FCCF's Family Life Minister. Granted, he was a licensed and practicing counselor, but several people wondered whether a victim of a church pastor would actually be okay with going to a session with a staff member of the church that hired the pedophile. FCCF posted the victim plan on the church website, along with a list of possible outside services and their hourly rates. However, the information was buried on the website, so casual observers or potential new members could not easily see it. It all appeared to be part of the protective mechanism that the elders and Steve Wingfield put into action to put protecting the church's image above helping the victims.

---

[101] https://restorefccf.org/elder-statement-7-26-15-to-the-congregation/

Here is the website text:

> Counseling for Victims of Sexual Abuse
> The initial counseling session is with First Christian
> On-site Licensed Professional Counselor Dennis
> Hounshell. Upon referral by Dennis, a secondary
> session will be performed by the recommended
> Outside Counselor. Those seeking counsel should call
> the church office (314-xxx-xxxx) or the confidential
> voicemail of Dennis Hounshell (314-xxx-xxxx).
>
> Counseling Cost Reimbursement
> Upon referral by the First Christian On-site Licensed
> Professional Counselor the church will cover costs
> incurred for the follow-up sessions for victims of
> sexual abuse related to Brandon Milburn and
> immediate family members.
>
> The church will pay all out-of-pocket fees for the first
> six (6) one-hour sessions and one half of all out-of-
> pocket expenses for the following six (6) sessions for a
> total of twelve (12) one-hour sessions. This
> reimbursement will either include the counselor's
> sliding fee scale or any co-pay for those using
> personal insurance.[102]

Julie Anne Smith of Spiritual Sounding Board took up the story in her blogs, reflecting on her own experience with church abuse. She voiced her dismay at how the elders chose to help the victims and questioned its efficacy.

> If YOU were a sex abuse victim and the pedophile who
> abused you was connected with the church...where leaders
> reportedly failed to notify authorities, would you feel
> comfortable going back to this church? ABSOLUTELY NOT!
> Going back to the place which represents harm would be the
> very last place you would want to go.

---

[102] https://restorefccf.org/first-christian-church-of-florissant-offers-counseling-for-victims/

Secondly, notice that it says the first session is with Licensed Professional Counselor, Dennis Hounshell. That means that the victims would have to relay their story first to Hounshell, and then get referred to another therapist. Going to one therapist is difficult enough. Imagine adding the sensitive sexual component on top of that. Part of the process of finding a counselor is establishing a level of trust. It is wrong to force a victim to go through these types of hoops. If a church is wanting to help financially, they should allow the victims to find therapists of their own choosing and then submit the therapy bills to the church. The church only needs to be involved only to establish that the victim is in fact receiving care from a licensed provider.

I'm not going to mince words here. It is my opinion that forcing victims to meet with Mr. Hounshell first, and then be transferring them to another therapist is re-victimizing. I would even go as far as to label it as emotional and spiritual abuse. The leaders of First Christian Church of Florissant are trying to control this therapy and it is not their place to do so. By interfering with the recovery process and forcing victims to go by their rules, church leaders are doing more destruction to these already shattered lives.[103]

The presumption that twelve sessions would fix the victims' issues frustrated and disappointed me. The man who made a six-figure salary offered church funds to cover not the fees for the sessions but only the out-of-pocket expenses. What might those expenses have been, a co-pay that insurance wouldn't cover?

So, there we have the story of the First Christian Church of Florissant. The church whose leadership chose all the wrong methods of handling sexual abuse in the church made the initial jab a gaping wound that could not be sutured or healed. Danny Wicentowski, who covered the story for the Riverfront Times, from the announcement of Brandon's arrest through Steve's return, expressed the tragedy of it all:

---

[103] Julie Anne, "A Closer Look at Ethical Issues Involving First Christian Church of Florissant and the Counseling They are Offering to Sex Abuse Victims," Spiritual Sounding Board, July 20, 2015, https://spiritualsoundingboard.com/2015/07/10/a-closer-look-at-ethical-issues-involving-first-christian-church-of-florissant-and-the-counseling-they-are-offering-to-sex-abuse-victims/.

And yet, in a sermon intended to trumpet a return to normalcy, Wingfield's explanations buried him deeper in the scandal that's taken his church to the brink. Wingfield may have missed the signs that his rising-star youth minister was grooming young boys for sex but suing whistleblowers and concerned congregants is what truly caused dissension in the congregation. And that went totally unaddressed.[104]

The timing of the body blows to the church all seemed to fall within the strange annual pattern of January to February from the time Dawn Varvil had her meeting with Steve and the executive minister in 2012. Brandon was arrested in February 2014 and pleaded guilty in February 2015. Steve, who sued members of his church family, potentially using money from the church family's donations to do so, returned to the pulpit to move on in February 2016. After Steve's reinsertion behind the pulpit at FCCF, the Truth and Reform FCCF members ceased their efforts toward the church and focused on the victims. They continued to meet weekly to worship. They hired Doug Lay for a small stipend to be the shepherd of their little flock. It helped him and his wife weather the loss of his job at SLCC. We also encouraged him in his fight on behalf of the victims.

Case #2

Allow me to introduce the main characters in this case: John Wayne (JW) Hinton, his son, Jimmy Hinton, and Somerset Church of Christ. JW was the senior pastor at Somerset Church of Christ, Somerset, PA, for about twenty-seven years. Somerset was a small church of perhaps sixty-five members. Jimmy went into the ministry as a young adult and eventually ended up as senior pastor at the same church he attended during his childhood. The time frames for the two churches coincide in the years between 2009 and 2011.

Jimmy had been the pastor at Somerset since June 2009. In July 2011, his sister disclosed an event from years before in which JW sexually abused her and a friend. She backed it up with an email between her and her friend. Feeling the intense weight she had borne all those years, Jimmy admired her bravery in revealing the secret.

---

[104] https://www.riverfronttimes.com/stlouis/after-six-months-away-pastor-at-center-of-church-cover-up-scandal-returns/Content?oid=3057702

When Jimmy discussed it with his mother, they decided to go to the police with the information. Consumed by the dread of the coming revelation to authorities, Jimmy struggled through the rhythms of scheduled events and responsibilities. He and his mother went together to speak with a detective. Their report was made anonymously but not without great anguish at the difficulty of doing the right thing.

> Mom and I had no game plan. How do you prepare to report the person who raised you? How on earth do you report your own father and best friend to the police. . .I reported my father because it was the right thing to do. My mom and I never entertained any other options . . . Mom and I had vital information that could both spare many new victims from abuse and put an abuser behind bars for the rest of his life.[105]

After a couple days of investigation, the detective called JW into the station for questioning. As she described it,

> Jimmy, he just left the station, and it's bad, it's really bad. There are many victims, and this is one of the worst cases of abuse I've ever had. Be expecting a call from him. He still doesn't know you were the one who reported.[106]

The next communication Jimmy heard from the detective was that his father had been arrested. She told him, "We've got your father in custody without incident. It won't be in the newspaper until Monday. Now is the time to tell your church."[107]

That is exactly what Jimmy did in a prepared statement to his congregation. He laid out the facts of the charges against their beloved pastor of almost three decades. He notified them that no one suspected wrongdoing until someone reported it to them. He owned up to his part as the reporting party, concluding,

---

[105]Hinton,618, 629.

[106] Ibid, 650.

[107] Ibid, 776.

. . . as a parent myself, I know the question all of you parents have right now. I cannot disclose names publicly because we need to protect victims. There is no question that any of you cannot ask me. I only ask that you ask me directly and verify everything with Officer Beckner. Please do not speculate with each other and add confusion to this situation. We need to work with facts and help victims and the church to heal.[108]

With that straightforward statement to his flock, he unified them into a team working together for the greater good of not only the victims but also the church. He put the priority on the victims and on an open discussion of the facts. He did not seek to protect the church's image or to hide behind his elders.

JW was subsequently convicted and sentenced to thirty years in prison.[109]

Then Pastor Jimmy entered a time of questioning. All the standard questions surfaced of "Why God? Where were you, God? How could you let this happen?" They triggered an intense need to figure out why his father did it. He began talking candidly with his father and studying the known tactics of abusers. He wanted to know how he chose his victims. He also wanted to know how his father kept under the radar of church members. The revelations he uncovered were astounding.

> In essence, instead of "looking for" abusers by identifying grooming behaviors, I wanted to start "looking for" us. Because that's exactly what abusers do. They're not interested in looking for other pedophiles. They're looking for us! Their lives are spent identifying victims to abuse, but they also need to find a community who will remain blind to the abuse. They are incredibly skilled and selective hunters. They instinctively know who to draw in closer and who to keep at arm's length. My dad recently told me that he could walk into any room, and within thirty seconds, he could identify the children he could potentially abuse and, at the same time, identify the most vulnerable adults who he could

---

[108] Ibid, 797.

[109] Randy Griffith, "Molester gets 30 years," *Tribune Democrat*, June 14, 2012, https://www.tribdem.com/news/local_news/molester-gets-30-years/article_6da7de4f-4bab-54ca-876d-67b3080da4c4.html.

manipulate into keeping blind to the abuse. Thirty seconds![110]

Pastor Jimmy turned this information into a healing balm for his church.

He and the congregation went through the stresses of publicity and the trial and struggled to move the church forward in their quest to teach the gospel. Yes, the flock diminished somewhat as a result of the incident, but those who remained found they could learn together and apply everything necessary to protect the flock. Now Jimmy travels, conducting training seminars for churches regarding all that he's learned.

> I get to see many details about what it takes to create the façade, select victims, and get away with abusing them. I view this as a once-in-a-lifetime opportunity to learn all that I can. It's the best way I know how to express to his victims that I care deeply about their souls and that their abuse will never be reduced to a shrug of the shoulder . . . The best way for our family, church and community to heal is to spend the time learning how abusers think and operate so that we can educate others and teach them how to quickly find high-risk individuals and fend them off.[111]

The Side-by-Side

With that overview of the Somerset Church of Christ, let me put the two cases side by side on the main issues facing both churches. Each of them had a duty to report the abuse, a duty for transparency to the church body, a duty to the victims, and a duty to make corrections within the church to make it safer for the people attending.

---

[110] Hinton, 1138.

[111] Ibid, 1224.

Case #1: First Christian Church of Florissant, Senior Minister Steve Wingfield	Case #2: Somerset Church of Christ, Senior Pastor Jimmy Hinton
Duty to report: Three people notified Steve Wingfield of the signs of potential abuse: a pastor, a parent, and a fire chief. Steve Wingfield did not report.	Duty to report: Pastor Hinton's sister came to him stating the abuse of her and a friend by JW Hinton. Pastor Hinton and his mother reported the incident immediately.
Duty for transparency: Elders made reactionary statements that included incorrect facts after the news broke of Brandon Milburn's arrest.	Duty for transparency: Pastor Hinton announced the arrest of JW Hinton in front of the church body prior to news reports.
Steve Wingfield sued the whistleblowers and included the church as a petitioner to silence them, which split the church body.	Pastor Hinton encouraged questions from his church family and opened the door for constructive conversations.
There was no internal investigation per Elder #5's statements in the leaders' meeting. Steve weaponized the elders against the Truth and Reform FCCF members.	Pastor Hinton opened himself and his family to the detectives' investigation. He began the journey to learn all he could about what it takes to become a predator and what it takes to defend the church body against them.
Steve hired men to "protect" him from anyone who questioned his actions. He used the police to intimidate those who wanted answers, serving them with orders of protection to lock them out of their church home.	Pastor Hinton loved on his flock as they walked together through the difficult days of hurt and anger.
Steve circled the elders around him to protect his image.	Pastor Hinton did not care about his image.

Duty to the victims: Steve and/or the elders contacted the family of one victim, according to Titus Benton's account. The church offered 12 hours of counseling with only out-of-pocket costs paid, but the victim had to speak to an FCCF minister first. The Family Life minister was fired upon Steve's return which meant the Family Life minister would not be at FCCF to see any victims.	Duty to the victims: Pastor Hinton requested that his church members refrain from speculation and adding confusion to the situation. He stated, "We need to work with the facts and help victims and the church to heal . . . A good leader will look into the faces of the victims and vow to defend and protect them."[112]
Duty to correct: FCCF increased security screenings for teachers and conducted short training meetings. No announcements came out regarding policy changes.	Duty to correct: Pastor Hinton wrote, "The best way for our family, church, and community to heal is to spend the time learning how abusers think and operate so that we can educate others and teach them how to quickly find high-risk individuals and fend them off."[113]

What if the voice of reason and responsibility made a difference at FCCF? Maybe it would sound like this from former Elder #1 written to the elders of FCCF:

> (From Elder #1)
> What would happen if the elders revealed to the congregation, a set of guidelines to be followed for a number of important issues?
>
> These issues might include the following list:
> - What if we observe unsettling physical contact between two students in our student ministry?
> - What if we observe unsettling physical contact between two children in our children's ministry?

---

[112]Ibid, 1632.

[113] Ibid, 1224.

- What if we observe unsettling physical contact between an adult and a student during any church-related occasion?
- What if we observe unsettling physical or emotional contact between an intern or staff member and another member, student or adult?
- What if we observe unsettling physical or emotional contact between members of staff or interns?
- What if we observe unsettling conduct of any type from an elder or minister?
- What if we have questions about actions taken by the elders or ministers?

Perhaps these issues might be clarified in an open congregational meeting. I think it's time to have greater candor and transparency, certainly on the current issue, and that might assist in establishing a continuing rapport with the congregation.

Thank you in advance for your timely response.

Really, what if the voice of reason and responsibility made a difference at FCCF? The church may have lost some members at the onset, but the mismanagement by Steve Wingfield and his elders shrank the church tenfold from 2,000 to 200 attendees. It could have helped the victims along on their lifetime of recovery, but instead the church revictimized them with their policy for counseling. Woe to the leadership at FCCF because the consequences of their actions are heavy.

Woe to the scatterer, "Woe to the shepherds who destroy and scatter the sheep of my pasture!' declares the Lord. Therefore, thus says the Lord, the God of Israel, concerning the shepherds who care for my people: 'You have scattered my flock and have driven them away, and you have not attended to them. Behold, I will attend to you for your evil deeds,' declares the Lord" (Jer. 23:1, ESV).

Woe to the one who wants to be greatest, who does not receive brothers and sisters but hinders those who do:

> I wrote something to the church, but Diotrephes, who wants to be first among them, does not acknowledge us.

Therefore, if I come, I will call attention to the deeds he is doing, disparaging us with evil words. And not being content with these, he does not receive the brothers himself, and he hinders those wanting to do so and throws them out of the church. Dear friend, do not imitate what is evil, but what is good. The one who does good is of God; the one who does evil has not seen God. (3 Jn.9–11, ESV)

Chapter 7: The Perishable

The Elders

I venture to say the elders suffered. Though they perpetuated spiritual abuse, some of it may have been a learned response after dealing with Steve Wingfield's abusive leadership for an extended period. I posit this not to excuse their behavior but to try to understand it. They brought about their downfall by blind obedience to the senior minister. From years in a conflicted marriage, I learned that placating a manipulative and abusive personality only perpetuates and exacerbates the problem.

> Truth did not prevail, because those who do not think as a sociopath do not understand the workings in the mind of the sociopath in front of them. Sociopaths, people with no intervening sense of obligation based in attachments to others, typically devote their lives to interpersonal games, to "winning," to domination for the sake of domination. The rest of us, who do possess conscience, may be able to understand this motivational scheme conceptually, but when we see it in real life, its contours are so alien that we often fail to "see" it at all.. . .We will doubt our own sense of reality first.[114]

> Listening and transparency — People in the congregation do not feel they really know Steve, and in any discussion where disagreement is brought forth, Steve has a tendency (an instinct really) to win every time. When concerns are brought, he may listen but then immediately discounts the input and rationalizes his view of it.[115]

Remember Elder #1's earlier comments?

> All of this to establish that the elders, particularly Elder #2, Elder #3, and I are making a mountain out of a mole hill. And he wondered why we didn't bring this stuff up in meetings upon which we said, almost with one voice, WE

---

[114] Martha Stout. *The Sociopath Next Door.* (Portland, OR: Broadway Books, 2005), 96.

[115] Elder #3 meeting notes email, dated Thursday, December 3, 2009.

HAVE TRIED AND YOU CUT US OFF AT EVERY TURN! So, we argued over that for a while, all the time being chided for thinking he chides us. (!@#$????@!!!!) Elder #2 committed to reform his behavior, and I said I would commit to working together with the elders as long as I could observe an effort on Steve's behalf to work with us without taking shots at us. Elder #3 didn't have to repent since he was not up for reelection.

This is what I mean: When the Milburn cover-up became known, there were, I believe, 7 elders, including SW, [Elder #9], [Elder #4], [Elder #6],[Elder #7], [Elder #5], and [the soon-to-be Executive Minister].The Sunday that the elders set for a Q&A in the lobby between services, [Elder #5] was an elder during the Q&A following the 8am Chapel service, but had resigned before the Q&A between the later services. As you witnessed, the elders were "in our faces" during the Small Group Leaders session, defending (SW = Steve Wingfield) and berating the members of the congregation who spoke up with honest and important questions.

Skip to the next "annual" congregational meeting where elders and deacons were to be confirmed (maybe December of 2015. . .? I don't remember being around for the election, so maybe it was spring of 2016.) Of those 7 elders, only (SW=Steve Wingfield), [Elder #6] & [Elder #4] remained. The others either resigned, were fired [the Executive Minister], or chose not to renew their position. [Elder #4] had planned to step down, but stayed, fearing there would be no one who could take on the financial mantle. So, 4 elders out of 6 left their posts (SW was elder by position). I've always wondered what precipitated this exodus since there was unwavering support earlier in the episode. Apparently, even SW couldn't hold their allegiance, or he actively sought to rid himself of them. As disheartening as this element is, I'm guessing not a handful in the congregation were really aware of this collapse in leadership.

The Church

From Lilly Fowler's article in the St. Louis Post-Dispatch:

> The church is still reeling from the recent conviction of
> Brandon Milburn, a former youth minister at the church
> who in March was sentenced to 25 years in prison for
> sexually abusing two young boys. Many members accuse
> Wingfield of mishandling the sexual abuse crisis at the
> church. They claim the pastor failed to report Milburn even
> after members brought the youth minister's questionable
> behavior to his attention, that he has done little to reach out
> to victims or seek out other potential victims, and that
> church leadership has done a poor job of communicating
> with members. "I am beyond frustrated at the way this has
> been managed and heartbroken that the church I once called
> home and love deeply has mishandled this situation so
> severely," Titus Benton, a former student minister at the
> church, said in a recent letter to church leadership. "First
> Christian has invited suspicion." Congregants further claim
> that the mismanagement of the situation is part of a larger
> pattern: Wingfield's authoritarian style leaves little room for
> discussion, and key staff members and dozens of families
> have fled. In fact, Wingfield sued several critics of the
> congregation in April, asking that they retract alleged false
> statements from social media.[116]

The church split that shot through the FCCF congregation caused seismic
cracks in the hearts of the brothers and sisters. There is no easy way to say,
"I love you, but I wholeheartedly disagree with you. I can no longer sit
under the teaching of this pastor." Pulling away from a church family is
like a divorce in that it leaves heartstrings dangling in the void.

FCCF struggled through low attendance and membership. Witnesses
attending said there were perhaps 200 (without taking an exact count) in
the sanctuary on the day Steve Wingfield returned to the pulpit. It was
such a sad day for those of us who had worked and prayed to rid FCCF of
the celebrity pastor who neglected his flock and allegedly failed to report
the abuser.

---

[116]Lilly Fowler, "The Battle for First Christian Church of Florissant," *St. Louis Post-Dispatch*,
June 8, 2015.

I supposed the phrase used in moving the church into the corporate template actually materialized—"You have to lose hundreds to gain thousands."

Martyn Lloyd-Jones, a well-known pastor and minister at Westchester Chapel in London for thirty years, stated his opinion on striving for numbers: "The great concern of the New Testament Epistles is not about the size of the church, it is about the purity of the Church."[117] Yet, in his own words, Steve Wingfield returned to the numbers game, judging his success by how many baptisms happened, as noted in the following First Christian Church in Florissant Facebook post, dated July 12, 2018:

> I admit it discouraged me when at invitation time Sunday, ZERO public decisions for Christ. (One of the first Sundays with no decisions since before Easter. Our highest was our church birthday in June when 8 people responded!) The good news is we've had several decisions mid-week in Starting Point and one teenager is being baptized today in Lake Michigan! Kyle sent the good news from our group of 25 teens at CIY Move conference in Chicago.

The quest for numbers continued.

What are the ramifications caused by this convergence of a perfect storm? What happened with the multi-million-dollar mortgage as church membership plunged from megachurch status to a tenth of the pinnacle membership in 2007 when Steve became senior pastor? Dwindling attendance translates to dwindling finances. The church building was sold to the Solomon Foundation and leased back to FCCF for a period of decades. The church now houses Grace Christian Academy to fill the empty rooms on weekdays. The church parking lot is still far from its packed status prior to six years ago. The people who invested for years to build the church and pay for its expansions no longer have a stake or a say in its future. I have no idea what happened to the notes that the church signed for personal loans from congregants at the time the worship center was constructed.

---

[117] https://virtueonline.org/lloyd-jones-heresy

The Whistleblowers

In their attempt to shed the light of truth on the circumstances surrounding the Brandon Milburn case, along with management problems at the church, the whistleblowers suffered. The accusations and lawsuits against them disrupted their lives and threatened their livelihoods. The apostle Paul asks a pertinent question:

> Have I then become your enemy by telling you the truth? They make much of you, but for no good purpose. They want to shut you out, that you may make much of them. (Gal. 4:16–17, ESV)

> For you were called to freedom, brothers. Only do not use your freedom as an opportunity for the flesh, but through love serve one another. For the whole law is fulfilled in one word: "You shall love your neighbor as yourself." But if you bite and devour one another, watch out that you are not consumed by one another. (Gal.5:13–14, ESV)

His home church and its elders sued Prof. Lay. They banned him from entering the church of which he was a member. Coerced into silence and spiritually abused by his employer, Doug Lay faced the life-changing decision to comply or stand for the victims. These were his employer's demands:

> Refrain from using social media, texting, email, or public media to espouse your cause (i.e. case study and Serious Answers for a Serious Problem) or criticize a local church (case study, etc.) as your job as professor obligates the college in matters of personal concern.

> Refrain from discussion of these matters with students or employees of St. Louis Christian College.

> Seek out opportunities for reconciliation to the best of your ability and depending on God with First Christian Church, Florissant relying on your conscience and God's Word as an ethical guide.

In other words, it boiled down to choosing between his seventeen-year career at the college and his duty to speak out against wrong. Prof. Lay chose the hard path of continuing to speak out on behalf of victims and against the church's cover-up. He chose not to sign the employment contract for another year at the college.

Meanwhile, Titus Benton fended off an effort by Steve Wingfield to have him fired from the church that he worked for in Texas. He and Kari continued their work at the church and started a nonprofit, *The 25 Group*, to raise money for needy communities around the world. Titus has since preached and worked at a couple of different churches while building *The 25 Group*. He is currently chief operating officer of an anti-trafficking organization in Houston and a candidate for public office. Kari serves her community as a nurse practitioner, loving on every person who comes through her door. They are succeeding despite the difficulty they faced in standing up for the victims and against the pastor and elders who they felt covered up for a sexual predator.

On June 26, 2015, Titus commented on the situation on the Spiritual Sounding Board website:

> As for our involvement, our courage and bravery pales in comparison to the courage and bravery of the young men who have stepped up, told their families and the newspapers what has happened to them. For that to be brushed aside, as if not reporting it were a communication error or a misunderstanding, is unacceptable and the genesis of our initial confrontation. Now, for those who have called foul on the church to be treated as they have been is nothing short of spiritual abuse. I'm not cool with that.[118]

Dawn Varvil moved away from Florissant and started a new job in 2021. She and her family struggled mightily through the personal comments against her and the lawsuit to silence her. Her demands to Steve Wingfield were brushed over in a letter from Steve's attorney.

---

[118]https://spiritualsoundingboard.com/2015/06/25/pastor-steve-wingfield-fail-to-report-child-sex-abuse/comment-page-1/#comment-278472.

Dawn, like all the whistleblowers, suffered a financial loss while legally defending her right to speak out. Supporters came together on a GoFundMe campaign to help with legal fees, which none of the whistleblowers could easily afford.

It is incumbent upon me to address the importance of the whistleblowers and the sacrifices they made to bring out the details of this sordid affair. It was the whistleblowers who held Steve accountable before his congregation and the public. I found a podcast by Julie Roys that fulfills my intentions. Here is a portion of the transcript of the November 12, 2020, episode of the Julie Roys Report in which she interviews Warren Cole Smith, senior fellow at the Colson Center and author of Faith Based Fraud.

> WARREN COLE SMITH 06:47
> And one of the things that I asked Stephen then was who provides accountability for him? Does he have deacons? Does he have elders? And he said something that stuck with me. He said, we're a staff led church. He does not have deacons and elders, at least they didn't at that time, I think that they have made some adjustments to the way they organize themselves since then. But even today, the bottom line is that there is very little accountability for someone like Steven Furtick. That experience opened my eyes to looking for that form of church government and church governance. So, what the fancy word for that is church polity in other churches, and I found it, unfortunately, to be common in the evangelical world. Mars Hill Church in Seattle, Washington, or at least it was in Seattle. That church has since gone away. In part because of the problems that they had there, was also a staff led church. The elders in that church were actually the staff members of that church. So unfortunately, I think what we're seeing today is a growth in megachurches, very large churches that are led by talented, gifted charismatic leaders like Steven Furtick, or, in the case of Mars Hill Church, Mark Driscoll, but men who have very little accountability. Folks who are not really in a position to say, Hey, dude, you need to do things differently here. Because the folks who are in a position to do that are usually people that are on the payroll of the church and can be fired by that senior pastor. And of course, it makes them very reluctant to speak up.

JULIE ROYS 20:42
And it fell apart because of a whistleblower. One man, that's
right, one man who took a look at the numbers and said,
Hmm, this isn't adding up. I don't know why we're doing
this. They started asking questions. And you know, as
Christian organizations are known to do, when he brought it
to his supervisors, and to those above him, they really didn't
think he was on to something because they trusted Mr.
Bennett. They trusted that he was doing the right thing. But
it shows how one man, and then one reporter, brought this
all to light. So describe what happened with that. It's a really
great story.

WARREN COLE SMITH 21:19
Well, it is a great story. And Albert Meyer is the man that
you're talking about. He was an accountant and a sort of an
adjunct part time professor at Spring Arbor College, a
Christian college in Michigan. Because Albert Meyer was
trained in accounting, and because he knew who Ponzi
was — the originator of the Ponzi scheme — it just didn't make
sense to him. It didn't add up. So he started paying
attention, started doing some research. And as you said, he
brought his concerns to the leadership of Spring Arbor
College. But at the time, they didn't want to hear because
they were making money. It was working for them. And in
fact, at one point, Albert Meyer thought that if he didn't
keep his mouth shut, he was probably going to lose his job.
And it was a job that he really needed because he was a
young man at that time. And he was, you know, supporting
a, you know, a growing family. Wasn't making a lot of
money. But he kept at it. He kept feeding information to
reporters. Finally, he got a reporter with The Wall Street
Journal, Steve Stecklo, to get interested in the story. And as a
consequence of that interest, a front-page story on the
Foundation for New Era Philanthropy was finally published
in The Wall Street Journal. Published in large part because of
the information that Albert Meyer was able to provide. And
that was ultimately what brought down the Foundation for
New Era Philanthropy. It's a great story of the courage and
the power of a single man, a whistleblower, who was willing
to tell the truth, despite circumstances that would have
caused a lesser person to buckle. And it's also by the way,

Julie, and this is where I take a lot of encouragement, and I think you should too, the power of journalism. The fact that even Albert Meyer might not have been able to make a difference if he was not able to get the attention of a newspaper. And it was the newspaper accounts made public that ultimately was the straw that broke the camel's back.[119]

The Victims

The tragedy is the victims. It's the victims who matter, not the threatened church image and income or the disgraced clergy and their tarnished witness. What is a victim? How do you identify a victim? Dictionary.com defines a victim as:

- a person who suffers from a destructive or injurious action or agency: a victim of an automobile accident.

- a person who is deceived or cheated, as by his or her own emotions or ignorance, by the dishonesty of others, or by some impersonal agency: a victim of misplaced confidence; the victim of a swindler; a victim of an optical illusion.

- a person or animal sacrificed or regarded as sacrificed: war victims.

- a living creature sacrificed in religious rites.

  Open your mouth for the mute, for the rights of all who are destitute. Open your mouth, judge righteously, defend the rights of the poor and needy. (Prov 31:8–9, ESV)

The victims were the silent watchers on the wall, waiting to see how the arrest and trial would turn out. They were the violated and emotionally damaged souls who lost the most and who have to deal with the hurt and the memories for the rest of their lives.

---

[119]Julie Roys, host, "Faith Based Fraud" Roys Report (podcast), November 12, 2020, accessed January 13, 2022, https://julieroys.com/podcast/faith-based-fraud/. Requested permission from the Roys Report Nov. 2, 2021.

The two boys who came forward for the trial in St. Louis County were not Brandon Milburn's only victims. There were six known victims in all. A third young man in Florissant chose anonymity. Two of the St. Louis victims attended Brandon's trial to present their impact statements, as reported in a May 6, 2015 news story in the Riverfront Times.

> The two victims, now college freshmen, walk to the dais to address the judge. (Riverfront Times has changed their names, and those of their families, to protect their identities.)
>
> "I stand before you a confused and hurt individual," says Adam Krauss, who first met Milburn through FCCF's children's ministry when he was in middle school. "Brandon Milburn was a guy I thought I could look up to and trust. He played a significant role in my spiritual life. He baptized me. . . He is a pathetic excuse for a man. He is a liar and a manipulator." (St. Louis Victim #1)
>
> Next up is Harris Anderson: His family allowed Milburn to live in its house for several months in 2007. Anderson, too, met Milburn through his family's connection to FCCF.
>
> "I kept the secret of what happened to me for seven years, seven very long years," he says, his voice shaking. "Your Honor, Brandon Milburn's effects on my life reach far past the sexual abuses of years ago. It seeps into my daily life even now. His actions broke my confidence, pride and trust." (St. Louis Victim #2)
>
> The two boys' parents took turns begging for consecutive sentences on each of the seven counts, what would amount to a true life-sentence.[120]

The third victim also spoke with the Riverfront Times. Reporter Danny Wicentowski added these comments to his May 6, 2015 article, garnered from an interview outside the confines of the courtroom. St. Louis Victim #3 did not speak at Brandon's trial.

---

[120] https://www.riverfronttimes.com/stlouis/a-youth-ministers-downfall-is-tearing-first-christian-church-of-florissant-apart/Content?oid=2772430

Nathan Rayner is sitting in a booth at St. Louis Bread Company (As with the other abuse victims quoted in this story, Rayner is not his real name.) As he lays out his history with Milburn, he uses roughly the same tone most people would use to describe the steps to make a salad. Dawn Varvil sits across the table, interjecting occasional details.

As Rayner tells it, Milburn first contacted him through Facebook when he was thirteen. He'd heard of Milburn through his churchgoing friends, so it's not like the college-aged man was a total stranger. Still, Rayner recalls, "He started asking me questions, started getting kind of personal. I didn't care. I was a sad kid—somebody cares, you know?"

Eventually, Milburn convinced Rayner to attend a service at FCCF. "I went back the next week, told him I wanted to get baptized," Rayner says.

Soon, Rayner was hanging around Milburn all the time, mostly at Varvil's house, joining the roughly 30 to 40 kids who made the home their unofficial hangout. It was a safe place, he says, away from a mother and stepdad who regularly threw him out of the house. Over the next year, Milburn and Rayner became inseparable, and the pattern established with the Andersons repeated itself: Milburn drove Rayner to church, treated him to Cardinals games and bought him gifts, including an iPad and iPhone. Milburn sent him constant text messages.

"I was kind of blinded," Rayner says.

Milburn found his own place in October, two blocks from Rayner's home. A different FCCF family helped Milburn move in and bought him appliances and furniture. Milburn gave Rayner a spare key.[121]

---

[121] Ibid.

Many years prior to the events in St. Louis, there were three other victims over several years in Brandon's hometown of Louisville. All three were close friends. All three knew Brandon and his family in a circle of friendship, as the families hung out together and worshiped together. They and their parents were granted the opportunity to express the deep confusion, hurt, and lasting guilt thrust into their lives by someone they knew and may have trusted at one time. I cannot adequately convey their story, but they wove their heartstrings into every word of their statements of impact to the trial judge.

> After realizing all this and still not being able to talk to or tell anyone of this past, I became very depressed. I suddenly wasn't good enough for anyone and everything I had ever done didn't matter because no one knew the real me. It was a dangerous depression, though. No one knew I felt this way, I was away at college on my own and had my own room where I could be left alone and pretend to my friends and family, when I saw them on occasion, that nothing was wrong. They didn't know that I laid awake in my dorm room haunted by my past and desperate for help and someone to talk to crying myself to sleep frequently and persistently yelling out to God. Why!? But, I couldn't show it. No one could know what had happened . . . The amount of pain and shame that he brought to my life and the people in it is something no human being should be capable of alone. He took full advantage of the trust of my family and the complexity of the relationships of the people involved between (Louisville Victim #2), (Louisville Victim #3), and myself. He convinced me that what he did was okay and attempted to again years later in a message on social media that (Louisville Victim #3) got as well. He has hurt people in ways that I didn't know people could be hurt and has single handedly ruined people and their reputations. He has broken people's lives and hearts that will never be able to be fixed. He put his parents in an unfathomable position and has completely ruined them as people (everyone here has witnessed it first-hand).[122]

---

[122] Letter from Louisville victim #1 to Judge Cohen, Dated March 5, 2015, entered into evidence March 6, 2015

The parents of Victim #1 wrote their thoughts to the judge, stating what other parents must ask themselves at the news of sexual abuse of their child.

Over the past thirteen months since this nightmare began, we have doubted ourselves as parents, beaten ourselves up wondering how we could have allowed this to happen to our son. We re-lived the past to see if there were any clues or red flags that we ignored. The strongest instinct parents have is to protect their children, and we had failed.

There is still concern as parents moving forward. Although he seems to be handling things OK, we worry about how he will deal with this issue in the years to come. Will it affect his future relationships, his ability to trust? We have constantly tried to talk with him and reassure him that this was not his fault. We have encouraged him to talk with us and seek counseling. It is our hope that the support of his family and his strong faith in God will carry him through the rough spots.

Looking back, it has become evident that Brandon is a master manipulator. It seems as though the sole purpose and focus of his life was to devise ways to put himself in positions where he had trusted access to young boys. He started at our local church where he easily gained the trust of adult leaders and parents, capitalizing on his family name and reputation. He readily volunteered at our church's summer camp, even getting special permission to do so when he was younger than the required age. He left Louisville to attend Bible College in St Louis where he quickly befriended families with young boys and worked with kids at a local church there. He then moved on to California where he reached out to at risk kids while working at a newly planted church. During this time, he accepted money from us to support him in his ministry. He also spoke at our daughter's wedding as our son stood in the sanctuary as a groomsman. His actions are the epitome of arrogance and masterful deceit.

Sadly, we believe that Brandon is a pedophile and would be a danger and a threat to young boys.

He has masterfully gained access to young boys and used his position as a minister to befriend them and use them to satisfy his perverse desires. He moved from city to city leaving a trail of destruction.

If there has been any solace during the past year it is that Brandon has been incarcerated and unable to molest any other children. As you ponder and determine his sentence, we urge you to consider the pain he has inflicted on all these young boys and their families. Brandon has not been forthcoming regarding any of the victims other than the ones who pressed charges, so who knows how many others there are? We owe a debt of gratitude to the boys who came forward and to their families for their courage. How many others are out there who have not found a way to come forward and be heard? Any time that Brandon serves behind bars is a short sentence compared to the lifetime of pain these boys and their families have and will endure.[123]

Louisville Victim #2 wrote his impact letter to the judge as well. The pain he expressed seared the page on which it was written.

But, Brandon saw this as an opportunity to take advantage of me . . . I was his sexual puppet, blinded by his lies, and trapped in a nightmare that I never fully understood. This was especially hard for me to live with as a kid, having to watch him live a lie everyday—considering he worked at the church and went on to graduate from Bible college, and became a children's minister. I grew up watching the rest of the world praise him for being a "man of god," when I was the only one who knew the real monster he actually was . . . Again, no words can describe the hurt and anger that I still deal with on a daily basis. But the main thing that I want to get across in this letter is how Brandon Milburn robbed me of my childhood and has made my life a living hell. He ruined any chance I had to have a normal relationship with my family. Along with me, he sexually abused two of my childhood friends, and still was not satisfied. He then moved to St. Louis to prey on new victims . . . And because of

---

[123] Letter from Louisville parents of victim #1 to Judge Cohen, entered into evidence March 6, 2015.

Brandon, now all us victims have to live with this horrible burden that we had no control over. Brandon Milburn is a sick individual.[124]

The parents of Louisville Victim #3 wrote:

That night, our world as parents completely changed. The heartbreak of this being done to our son, and him dealing with it on his own for so many years has been almost unbearable. It is so hard for us to look at childhood pictures and realize what our son was going through. We have known Brandon since his birth. He was best friends with our oldest daughter until about age 14. He basically cut off friendships with people his own age and started spending most of his time volunteering at our Church, with elementary age children. He would later spend 3 summers volunteering at our Church Camp. He would spend several weeks there each summer. The potential for other victims there is frightening. As we look back, we realize how premeditated and calculating he was. He was loved at our Church. He professed a desire to go into the Ministry, and by doing so had everyone convinced he was a great kid and role model.

Brandon Milburn is a very dangerous man and we still lose sleep at night thinking about all the possible victims there are. He has fooled so many people using God, Faith and Churches, and left so much devastation in his path. After much research we now know he is the classic profile of a pedophile. He has truly affected our entire family, not only in the present but into the future as well.[125]

The thoughts of the abused turn inward against the thinker. More times than not, the thoughts and suffering remain unspoken, and victims berate themselves to the point of self-harm.

---

[124] Letter from Louisville victim #2 to Judge Cohen, Dated March 5, 2015, entered into evidence March 6, 2015

[125] Letter from Parents of Louisville Victim #3 to Judge Cohen, Dated March 1, 2015, entered into evidence March 3, 2015.

Received this note from an abuse survivor who gives each of us a difficult glimpse into the pain and lies so many survivors struggle with each day. Her brave words are also a stark reminder of how our culture is often the source of her pain and struggle.

This friend is one of the real heroes. . .

One HUGE piece of why many of us stay silent, is b/c our perpetrators are SO "perfect." We are not. We (the universal we) struggle with failed suicide attempts, cutting, eating disorders, PTSD, anxiety, depression, etc. Our offenders are perfect and blameless. They wear suits and ties, have the perfect haircut, the perfect charm. They are those with stellar reputations, those with a long list of successes—no struggles that would give them labels, etc.

I don't have a family that will support me. I (and the other victims) are pretty much on our own as far as defending our reputations. There are many who can gain from trying to make us look un-credible and they are all powerful, respected people.

We are nobodies. . .just regular people, but people who are struggling to live in healthy ways after being raised in horrific environments.[126]

Let the voices of the victims once silenced by manipulation and shame ring out in triumph and healing. What is it about this destruction that Steve Wingfield and the elders of FCCF did not get? How could they ever think that twelve hours of counseling could right the wrongs done to these boys? The deeper I go into this investigation, the greater my anger grows at the irresponsibility of those whom I thought to be godly men. They were not. They cannot convince me their actions were godly in any way, shape, or form. They did only enough to cover for their bad choices throughout the cascade of incidents. This statement from Doug Lay's attorney in the form of a press release on May 20, 2015, sums up my thoughts:

---

[126]GRACE – Godly Response to Abuse in the Christian Environment, July 5, 2016. https://www.facebook.com/netgraceorg/

Doug Lay and his attorney, Al W. Johnson, believe that there are many sincere and decent people at the First Christian Church of Florissant. Unfortunately, Pastor Steve Wingfield and the current leadership of the Church have failed in their leadership duties to their members as well as to the victims of Mr. Milburn's horrific crimes.

Chapter 8: The People in the Pews

I've wrestled with the logic of those who stayed at FCCF. There's a truth in the saying that "ignorance is bliss." How can someone know the water is sour if they haven't tasted it? Many church members weren't at the meetings for leaders and parents. Many hadn't seen the issues that those of us who pushed to restore FCCF experienced personally. Many never experienced Steve Wingfield's disdain. Years ago, I lived with my family in one of the units owned by my parents-in-law. The water supply consisted of a cistern that stored city water for use by several units, including the one we occupied. At one time the water became bitter, and I worried about its safety. Yet, my concerns were brushed off when I complained to my father-in-law about it. That is, until he drank some of the water while working outside the units. The problem got fixed that day. Some people don't comprehend until they have tasted the water themselves.

The few hundred congregants who chose to stay hadn't tasted the bitter water, so they continued to see only the exterior persona of Steve Wingfield. Perhaps they saw and experienced his underlying nature but chose to stay anyway. A dear friend and fellow choir member who was part of the small group I attended for years was the only one among our small group who decided to continue attending FCCF. She felt led by the Holy Spirit to stay. Perhaps she believed she could help bring the church to restoration by staying. She was a main contributor to the church. She was among the influencers invited to the Wingfields for their fund-raising events. Perhaps she felt she had so much invested in the church after all the years of her membership that she just couldn't leave. She never explained her decision any further than not being called to leave, which is a valid enough reason. Though we continued meeting together in the small group, we lost the closeness of worshipping and serving together.

Some of the longtime members, even elders and prominent members, recorded their reasons for leaving FCCF on a website set up by the restoration group's steering committee. Here are the most relevant.

> SL: The elders were "trained" by Steve Wingfield that their main role in spiritual oversight of the church was to support the lead minister (Steve) and pray for him and his family . . . to "have his back." I was among a few other elders who fought to have Steve held accountable for his actions, but

our concerns at that time had nothing to do with the sexual abuse by Brandon Milburn — none of that had yet come up on anyone's radar. The actions we were concerned with were related to Steve's abusive management of staff and volunteers . . . During this time, the elders were being told that they shouldn't talk to any staff without Steve present, and the staff were forbidden from talking to any elder . . . When it became clear to Steve that we were not giving up, he began his efforts to take control away from the elders. A specialist was brought in to teach us about a new "governance model" that was supposed to position us for megachurch growth. The real effect was to get the elders out of the way. This new model, based on the Carver Policy Governance model, would put the senior minister in total control of the staff, and take the elders officially out of the picture. The elders' role would be to provide the spiritual oversight, project the vision for the ministry and supervise the senior minister. The senior minister would be "the CEO" and the elders would be "the board of directors." The main thing was that the elders would have NO interaction or involvement with staff, other than Steve . . . In addition, he took steps to institute new selection criteria for incoming elders to ensure they were already in agreement with him and took steps to oust the elders already on the board who were standing in his way. I ultimately resigned when I saw that this was the course of action the elders as a group were going to go along with. I could not be a part of allowing this to happen.

Former Staff Member #1: I also felt like I was being forced to continue to do things that were no longer working, because they were run by family and/or because it was something we had always done. The environment was very difficult to work in and it got to the point where we felt we could not effectively minister to our students because we were constantly so frustrated. A second reason we left was because of the "ALL IN" campaign. We could not get behind the tens (and even hundreds) of thousands of dollars that were to be spent on LED signs and bathroom remodels when we had a community hurting so deeply and when we were still in 6 million dollars of debt on our building.

Former Staff Member #2: Steve was a manipulative micromanager and made it very hard for me to use my gifts and talents for the kingdom. Nothing was ever good enough, and if staff openly praised my work in our staff meetings, he would reprimand me in private that it doesn't matter what others think—all that matters is what he wants. I thought the issue was with me and not him—he's the senior pastor after all... I don't believe the elders are competent. It seems like Steve has surrounded himself with a group of Yes-Men with no backbones that are blinded by Steve's deity-like status at the church. In my mind, the elders should be removed, and the congregation should vote in new elders, and Steve CANNOT be one of them.

Former Member #1: However, as to why we left, it boils down to a few things. 1) We lost respect for the elders who in our opinion failed to hold Steve accountable. 2) We lost respect for the ministers who in our opinion chose to remain @ FCCF knowing the dysfunction and choosing to do nothing about it. 3) We lost respect for Steve who in our opinion knowingly lied and deceived the ministers, elders and congregation, all who were unwilling or unable to question anything that came out of his mouth for fear of retribution.

Former Member #2: All I can say is...he's had a really hard time over the last several years determining who the wolf is. First, it was undeserved church discipline for a minister. Then, it was non-compete contracts to protect "his" members from hungry staff who might leave "his" church and take "his" members.

Next, it was members (including my husband and myself) who asked questions and were told half-truths and full lies, but were told to get on board or leave. During this time, another staff member/youth volunteer was receiving the highest praises and recommendations from him, all the while preying on young boys who attended the church. He was told that this staff member/youth volunteer was sleeping in the same bed with a young boy in a compromising position and also exposing himself to young boys and having them expose themselves back. Yet, this staff member/youth volunteer remained and was free to continue to "minister" with the youth and children. And this staff member/youth volunteer was given recommendations by him to go to other churches to "minister." Then, it was restraining orders and lawsuits and church bans for members who were asking questions about the one who was preying on children. Something's messed up here. . .who is the wolf again?

Former Member #3: at the time Steve Wingfield went out on sabbatical: Again, I am nowhere near trusting the elders again at this point and it will take a lot to change that, but I'm at least trying to consider the possibility that their plans are more in line with our hopes than they feel like they can publicly communicate. Thoughts?

Former Member #4: I'm very concerned that nothing was said or even alluded to that maybe just maybe the elders might have made a mistake or two and need to ask for forgiveness. The same goes for W (Wingfield), the elders see no reason why he needs to ask for forgiveness. Oh, sure maybe he's made a small mistake here or there in dealing with a few staff but he's not that bad and he'll be back having received help for all the stress and heartache the rest of us have caused. For the ban to be lifted, Muellers, Lays, and Bentons must ask for forgiveness. There again, they made all the mistakes W (Wingfield) and the elders were the victims. I also feel for Dennis because he put himself out there yesterday asking people to come back then the rug was pulled out from under him by the reading of the latest nonsense. If the elders want to prove they are going to start being Biblical elders they had better show it soon.

My personal opinion from having gone through this experience is multi-dimensional. Steve Wingfield failed:

- His elders. He set himself above them and in total control of them. Judging from their comments, it appears that he refused to submit to their counsel. Instead, he used them as a protective posse to buffer him from conflict. As one of the elders, Steve failed himself. In his effort to protect his image, he eroded the respect and confidence he might have had from his congregation.

- His church. He let the wolf through the doors. He did not guard his flock from the predator, and then he verbally and spiritually abused his members.
- Individual members of his church, people who had contributed tithes and offerings since before he assumed leadership. He banned some from church property. He sued his supporters. He tried to silence the truth of the whistleblowers.
- The victims, which is perhaps the most egregious failure of all.
- Me as a partaker in Christ, which leads me to say that he may have educational credentials, but he does not have the Biblical credentials to be my senior minister.

Chapter 9: The Purpose

What value is all of this to the Body of Christ? What are the takeaways that can promote healing and prevent others from getting wrapped up in another potentially explosive church situation?

The Church cannot escape having to deal with sexual abuse threats. It can, however, do everything within its power to prevent predators from sneaking into the body. Some say the church is the safest place for children, but my research shows me that is not true. I believe God's people can make a difference by taking a stand for truth and by being the church that Christ leads. Can we take a stand for victims? Can we set aside the fear of a tarnished church image and work together? Can we bolster the security of our youth with training for the keepers of the gates and the teachers? Can we allow questioning of pastors, elders, and policies? Can we demand transparency from our leaders? Can we be watchful and not allow ourselves to vote for something simply because the elders say we should trust them?

The exercise of searching through the myriad documents, articles, letters, testimonies, and sources brings me to make my purpose statement. The purpose of this writing is to take a stand for victims before they become victims.

> Abusers easily prey on the naivety of religious folks, including church leaders. . . What abusers don't expect is for Christians to think like someone who lives a double life, while pretending to be naïve . . . Once an abuser introduces himself to a parent of a target child, all he has to do is create the reality and values that those parents want or expect to see in others . . . Abusers are masters of deception and manipulation and will wear their victims down.[127]

The fact that a church gets so big that the senior minister doesn't recognize the Sunday school teacher who has taught his flock for more than two years is a red flag. Is this an inherent failure of the megachurch? Has the senior minister distanced himself so far from the flock that he has lost track of who belongs to it?

---

[127] Hinton, 1247, 1401, 1453, 1886.

Let us be the Church that Christ leads by following the wisdom of his Spirit-breathed Scriptures.

> And he gave the apostles, the prophets, the evangelists, the shepherds and teachers, to equip the saints for the work of ministry, for building up the body of Christ, until we all attain to the unity of the faith and of the knowledge of the Son of God, to mature manhood, to the measure of the stature of the fullness of Christ, so that we may no longer be children, tossed to and fro by the waves and carried about by every wind of doctrine, by human cunning, by craftiness in deceitful schemes. (Eph. 4:11–14, ESV)

Let us rise to the occasion and take a stand for victims. Let us go out to gather their brokenness as a church and see to the needs of our brothers and sisters. After thirteen years in recovery ministry, I've come to love Isaiah 58:6–8, ESV.

> Is not this the fast that I choose:
> to loose the bonds of wickedness,
> to undo the straps of the yoke,
> to let the oppressed go free,
> and to break every yoke?
> Is it not to share your bread with the hungry
> and bring the homeless poor into your house;
> when you see the naked, to cover him,
> and not to hide yourself from your own flesh?
> Then shall your light break forth like the dawn,
> and your healing shall spring up speedily;
> your righteousness shall go before you;
> the glory of the Lord shall be your rear guard.

Andrew (Jake) McDonnell contrasts the gospel approach to the wrong approach in a letter he forwarded to the congregation, which he titled "Return to the Gospel First Christian Church of Florissant and St. Louis Christian College."

> To the family and leadership at First Christian Church of Florissant and to the administration at St. Louis Christian College:

How does a leader react when they know people have been victimized?

Gospel Approach: Leaders react with compassion, honesty, and love. As Jesus did and does, they seek out those who are hurting and call forward all those who are burdened, even to the ends of the earth (Luke 19:10). They advocate for victims and champion care for the marginalized (James 1:27).

And, they reach out to the evil person and perpetrator of the crimes, in order to share the truth of the redemption Jesus Christ offers to them as well. (And, this was what Doug Lay did when Milburn was taken into custody. I have read that this was also the case with FCCF. If the purpose of the many visits from FCCF people to Milburn was for the sake of ministry to him, I commend you. That was done in accordance with the gospel (Matthew 5:43–48).)

Wrong Approach: Leaders with a wrong approach ignore and neglect victims and possible victims in their own midst and call it "honoring" them by "allowing them to initiate communication and process healing through the counselors of their choosing."

They call themselves the victim and attempt to paint those who point out their unrepentant sin as oppressors, taking attention away from the only true victims of the crime and manipulating the situation for their own safety and/or gain.

They shift blame away from themselves by saying "the criminal acts that took place in 2007 did not occur in our facility or as part of our programming . . ." or insinuate that the person who hired the perpetrator is really responsible for his behavior by saying "I did not supervise Brandon, [the hiring] was [Benton's] personal request."

They shift blame away from themselves by purposefully and deceptively minimizing the perpetrators involvement in the church in public statements. This is manipulation and deception, not the work of a minister or ministers of the gospel.[128]

Let the church indeed return to the gospel and let Bible colleges include classes to prepare pastors to protect their flocks from predators.

> Conversations of deception and abuse in the church were completely absent from my training . . . But I think most, if not all, seminaries in our country are failing to equip ministers to distinguish wolves from sheep. We are pretending that churches are safe when they are not. Nothing—and I mean absolutely nothing was taught about screening or background checks. Not a word was taught about the prevalence of sexual abuse in the church or the need to have a written policy.[129]

---

[128] https://restorefccf.org/return-to-the-gospel-first-christian-church-of-florissant-and-st-louis-christian-college/

[129] Hinton, 461, 472, 508.

Chapter 10: Postlude

Six years have passed since the height of the storm at FCCF. Here are significant events that have taken place since.

- The Department of Education notified St. Louis Christian College of the negative findings of a program review report issued by the US Department of Education's School Participation Division in Kansas City, which was dated April 8, 2015. This is, interestingly enough, the same date that FCCF's elders, including Steve Wingfield, held their raucous meeting with church adult class teachers and recovery ministry leaders. Yes, the one that gave me flashbacks. According to this letter, SLCC was in trouble as far back as 2013, as the date on the findings report is November 4, 2013.

    > Final determinations have been made concerning all of the outstanding findings of the program review report. The purpose of this letter is to notify SLC of the Department's final determinations and to notify SLC of a possible adverse action. Due to the serious nature of Findings 1, 2 and 3, this FPRD is being referred to the Department's Administrative Actions and Appeals Service Group (AAASG) for its consideration of possible adverse administrative action pursuant to 34 C.F.R. (Section) 668, Subpart G. Such action may include a fine, or the limitation, suspension or termination of the eligibility of the institution.

- The Department of Education levied a huge fine on SLCC for failing to comply with federal standards. SLCC received a detailed explanation dated June 13, 2017. I am not aware of what the college sent to the DOE in response to these notices.

    > As detailed in this letter, SLC's violations of the Clery Act, the fire safety requirements in the HEA, the DFSCA, and the Department's regulations are very serious and numerous. SLC's students and their families, and the institution's employees must be able to rely on the disclosures of campus crime and fire safety statistics, policies and statements to understand

the extent of crime and fires on campus and the institution's security policies. Congress enacted the DFSCA to ensure that students and employees had vital information about the DAAPP at their institution. Moreover, a DAAPP that has not been tested in a biennial review is unlikely to be reliable and effective. SLC's students and employees were not given information about the standards and code of conduct expected of them with regard to drug and alcohol use, and the sanctions that could be imposed if the code of conduct is violated. Moreover, the Department considers an institution's compliance with the Clergy Act, and the DFSCA requirements to be part of its administrative capability, and SLC's failure to comply with those requirements constitutes an inability to properly administer the Title IV programs.

After considering the gravity of the violations and size of the institution, I have assessed a fine of $15,000 for SLC's failure to publish and properly distribute a complete and accurate ASR for calendar year 2012. The publication and distribution of the ASR is a fundamental requirement of the Clery Act. The ASR provides important safety and security information to the institution's students and employees, and prospective students and employees so that they can appropriately assess an institution's security. Thus, the failure to provide this information is a serious violation of the Clery Act.

I have assessed a fine of $15,000 for SLC's failure to publish and properly distribute a complete 2012 AFSR. This is a serious violation because the campus community and the public were deprived of important information to help them make important safety decisions with regard to fire safety at SLC. This violation is similar to the failure to publish an ASR.

I have assessed a fine of $15,000 for SLC's failure to develop and implement a substantive DAAPP, properly distribute a DAAPP disclosure to all employees and students enrolled for academic credit on an annual basis, and failure to conduct a biennial review to evaluate the effectiveness of its DAAPP and to assess the consistency of sanctions imposed for violations of its disciplinary standards and codes of conduct related to drugs and alcohol. This is a serious violation because students and employees cannot be expected to benefit from a drug and alcohol prevention program that is deficient and has not been properly distributed to them. Moreover, students and employees cannot be expected to rely on a DAAPP that has not been tested for its effectiveness.

The fine of $45,000 will be imposed on July 3, 2017, unless I receive, by that date, a request for a hearing or written material indicating why the fine should not be imposed. SLC may submit both a written request for a hearing and written material indicating why a fine should not be imposed.[130]

- Discussions of SLCC's merger with Central Christian College of the Bible in Moberly, Missouri, took place at the October 2021 meetings.[131] As stated in the description of proposed changes, the Solomon Foundation came back into play in this end point of the St. Louis Christian College era: "Any agreed plan will then be implemented during the following months with the support of The Solomon Foundation and other regional partners."

- A St. Louis victim filed a personal injury lawsuit against Steve Wingfield and the church. "The new lawsuit similarly describes Seppelt's attempt at the time to alert Wingfield to what he had seen in Joplin in 2011; the suit notes, 'Neither Defendant Wingfield, nor FCCF personnel chose to report Milburn to Child Protective Services, fire him, or supervise him more closely following this

---

[130] Letter to SLCC President Pabarcus from The United States of America Department of Education, June 13, 2017, OPE-ID: 01258000.

[131] "Better Together," St. Louis Christian College, https://stlchristian.edu/merger/.

incident."[132] The motion for the hearing was filed on November 8, 2021, by the complainant's attorney. A hearing is set for the end of April 2022. The complainant is asking for a jury trial. Could this be the end of the FCCF era as well? Perhaps this could be the end of the Wingfield family dynasty at FCCF. Like my reference to starting over after a divorce, perhaps this will be a chance to change the guard at FCCF, leading to a new beginning based soundly on the gospel.

Thank you for your attention to the story of a broken church. As part of my quest to make this piece meaningful to victims, I have selected a nonprofit organization in St. Louis to which a portion of the profits from this writing will be sent. God's justice has been adjudicated against the perpetrator. He has used governmental agencies to bring down the college. He may also use the victims' bravery to bring justice to the church and to Steve Wingfield. It's time to get the victims into the forefront of the picture.

Safe Connections
2165 Hampton Avenue
St. Louis, Missouri 63139

---

[132] Danny Wicentowski, "Victim Sues St. Louis Church of Former Youth Minister Convicted of Sex Abuse," *Riverfront Times,* October 28, 2021, https://m.riverfronttimes.com/newsblog/2021/10/28/victim-sues-st-louis-church-of-former-youth-minister-convicted-of-sex-abuse.

Appendix

"Is It Enough?" Sexual Abuse Within the Church: A Case Study at First Christian Church of Florissant Joy 6th Edition. March 28, 2015.

Introduction[133]

He was a Bible College graduate, a skilled musician, a talented worship leader, a gifted creative arts director, a youth sponsor, a church intern, a church member — and a child molester.

On January 26, 2015, in a courtroom in St. Louis County, Brandon Milburn pleaded guilty to seven counts of sodomy with two minors under the age of 12 — two innocent, impressionable, and trusting boys from a North County church. He awaits his sentencing on March 30, 2015, a sentence that could bring 10 years to life.

But that is not the end of the story, nor is it the beginning of the story — it is the middle of the story.

The Churches 1

First Christian Church of Florissant

The beginning of the story goes back to a time when Brandon first arrived in St. Louis. He enrolled at Saint Louis Christian College[134] in August of 2005 and began attending and volunteering with the children's ministry at FCCF. The church hired Brandon part-time as a children's intern with two other interns the next year (2006), working with 5th graders. He would continue as a paid intern through December of 2007.

During the 2006 — 2007 school year, a former staff member reported that

---

[133] Because this document was included as an exhibit in a lawsuit brought by Steve Wingfield and First Christian Church of Florissant against three others and me on April 16, 2015, this document is now in the public record. Although the lawsuit was dropped without prejudice on May 11, 2015, the plaintiffs are still allowed to reopen the lawsuit within the statute of limitations.

[134] Saint Louis Christian College https://stlchristian.edu/.

"I had conversations with Brandon about being alone with both (Family Name) boys and the youngest (Family Name) as all 3 boys stated how uncomfortable they had gotten. Not to my surprise, he pushed what I was saying away. I told the (Family Name) about my conversation and how uncomfortable their son was and they asked Brandon to move back to SLCC. From there, I honestly avoided him...because he honestly, avoided me."[135]

In June of 2007, Brandon committed the six accounts of sodomy against two young boys under the age of 12. It would be four months later, in October of 2007, that Brandon committed the seventh count of sodomy.

No one knew except the two innocent victims — and Brandon.

We now know — so as the steps of Brandon's story are retraced, we hope it may help to interpret the "circumstantial" evidence to better understand and learn from this tragic event.

Southeast Christian Church

Brandon left town after graduating from SLCC in December of 2007 and returned to his hometown of Louisville, Kentucky. He was employed at Southeast Christian Church[136] as an Atmosphere and Media Tech from October of 2008 to April of 2009.[137]

First Christian Church of Florissant

Brandon returned to St. Louis to re-enroll at SLCC in August of 2009 to pursue a BS degree in preaching. He returned to First Christian Church of Florissant to volunteer and work with the youth — and to return to the two minors he had abused in 2007.

---

[135] Facebook Message March 17, 2015.

[136] Southeast Christian Churchhttps://www.southeastchristian.org/

[137]Linked In
https://www.linkedin.com/start/join?trk=login_reg_redirect&session_redirect=https%3A%2F%2F
www.linkedin.com%2Fprofile%2Fview%3FauthType%3DNAME_SEARCH%26locale%3Den_
US%26srchtotal%3D3%26trkInfo%3DVSRPsearchId%3A4063682681

It was during his first semester back at SLCC that Brandon would bring minors from the church over to his dorm. One[138] of the Resident Assistants said,

> "I had noticed that Brandon had been bringing junior high and high school students back to the dorm to hang out in the lounge or in his room. Honestly, I didn't get a weird feeling about it at all. I figured he was spending time with them in a positive way. However, I did encounter him having the door shut with a junior or senior high boy in the room. I always had an open door policy on my floor (meaning that I left my door open if I was there)."

> "I decided after that evening I needed to approach Brandon about what I had witnessed. I didn't expect anything at all; I simply felt that no underage student should be allowed to be behind a closed door for any reason in a dorm."

> "I shared what I expected from Brandon and he said, "Oh yeah, that's probably a good call" and from that day on we never had a problem (that I was aware of). However, in 2010 Brandon would hardly spend any time in the dorms or on campus."

One of Brandon's roommates witnessed the same behavior:

> "I can only remember a handful of times that he ever brought a youth to the dorm rooms. They never stayed for more than a minute or two. I was always there before they were. I don't remember ever walking in and finding him with a student. I can't ever remember actually seeing anything suspicious while I was rooming with him."[139]

Another RA summarized a very common observation made by his fellow dorm mates,

---

[138] Facebook Message on February 20, 2015.

[139] Facebook Message on February 20, 2015.

"He lived with some families from the church off and on while I was at SLCC. This was the only suspicious thing for me and that's probably too strong a word for what I thought at that time. It was just a little strange that he spent much of his time off campus with students and families from his church and so little time with his peers on campus."[140]

Discovery Church

The following summer, 2010, Brandon served as an intern at Discovery Church[141] in Simi Valley, California.

While at that church, Brandon met a young woman. She enrolled at SLCC for the spring semester of 2011. She told me one day after class that although she had received offers from other colleges, she turned them down to attend SLCC for one main purpose—to be with Brandon. He, however, was not interested—a sentiment he repeated every time I asked him about her. He would often say that he just wanted to focus on his relationship with the Lord and ministering to the kids at church instead. I believed him.

First Christian Church of Florissant

Brandon returned to SLCC in August of 2010. His roommate during his last year[142] at the college summarized how most students perceived him, "He (Brandon) was known as the invisible man."[143] Concerning Brandon's relationship with young boys, he said that he "admired how he (Brandon) brought students under his wings" and how "he brings them along when he was working or when he was on stage."[144]

Brandon graduated in August of 2011 with a BS degree in preaching.

---

[140] Facebook Message on February 21, 2015.

[141] Discovery Church http://discoverychurch.com/

[142] August of 2010 to May of 2011.

[143] Phone interview on March 4, 2015.

[144] Phone interview on March 4, 2015.

In August of 2011, Brandon was hired by FCCF as the Creative Elements Director, a position he held until January of 2012[145] although he was still listed on the FCCF website as the CED as of February 16, 2012.[146]

It was during a two-day mission trip to tornado ravished Joplin in August of 2011 that I first noticed "something unusual" about Brandon. He was part of a group of members from FCCF who had traveled to Joplin to help with the cleanup. Brandon had been asked by the church to provide video coverage of the trip, something for which he was profoundly talented. Yet, during filming one day, I observed that a young boy, about 14 years old, was constantly following Brandon. They had traveled to Joplin separately from our group in the church van; they had traveled together back to St. Louis in a separate car. The minor was quiet and reserved, often looking away from me if I tried to speak to him. I forgot about it until six months later.

Since this trip, one of the church members on that trip recently told me of an inappropriate incident between Brandon and the minor. The men from the church were spending the first night in Joplin at a large facility, including Brandon and the minor. Located in the corner, was a long counter, similar to a bar counter. This church member said that Brandon and the minor were sleeping next to each other behind this counter while the other men were sleeping out in the open. He confronted Brandon and told him it was inappropriate. Brandon replied that the minor was afraid of sleeping in front of adults. When the group returned to St. Louis, this church member informed the senior minister at FCCF about the incident.[147]

[145] Linked In
https://www.linkedin.com/profile/view?id=138428543&authType=NAME_SEARCH&authToken=VM_d&locale=en_US&srchid=4063682681425149403848&srchindex=1&srchtotal=3&trk=vsrp_people_res_name&trkInfo=VSRPsearchId%3A4063682681425149403848%2CVSRPtargetId%3A138428543%2CVSRPcmpt%3Aprimary

[146] First Christian Church of Florissant
https://web.archive.org/web/20120216192449/http://www.fccf.org/welcome/ministry-staff/

[147] Phone conversation on March 24, 2015.

Gateway Christian Church

At the end of January of 2012, Brandon left FCCF and was hired on a contract basis to do graphic art design, to participate with the worship team on Sundays, and to run sound at Gateway Christian Church[148] in St. Louis, a job that was similar to what he had done at FCCF. He was hired by the worship minister[149] on a contract basis, not as an employee of the church.[150] This was my second "something unusual" moment. Brandon was exceptionally talented as a speaker, musician, artist, and techie. Churches would always be highly interested in someone with Brandon's skills—so why would Brandon leave a church with over 1000 members to work at a much smaller church down the street?

While Brandon worked at Gateway on Sunday mornings, he continued to volunteer with the youth group at FCCF on Wednesday evenings. This continued from February to May of 2012. This was my third "something unusual" moment. Why did Brandon leave his employment at FCCF but continue to volunteer on Wednesday evenings with the youth at the church where he was no longer employed? Each of these "something unusual" moments seemed insignificant by themselves, but they soon were about to be connected—the beginning of the end for Brandon.

Mission Church

After Brandon completed his contractual agreement at Gateway Christian Church sometime in May of 2012, he headed west to another church, this time in Ventura, California. When he first arrived, he posted a video, created by himself, of a young male skateboarding with Brandon at Moor Skate Park in California.[151] It appears that Brandon began attending and/or working at Mission Church,[152] possibly as early as July 8, 2012.[153]

---

[148] Gateway Christian Church, http://gccstl.org/.

[149] He is no longer the worship minister at Gateway CC. He is currently the worship leader at FCCF, and the son-in-law of the senior minister.

[150] Phone interview with the senior minister at Gateway CC on March 3, 2015.

[151] 2 Go CamerasMoor Skate Park, https://vimeo.com/43318414.

[152] Mission Church, http://missionventura.com/gallery/home/.

[153]Twitter, July 8 2012, https://twitter.com/brandoburn/status/222017111818633217.

One of Brandon's roommates remembered that Brandon had left Mission church sometime before April of 2013 and that he had spent some time at a ranch—some type of treatment center—outside of California, but Brandon did not tell the roommate for what type of treatment.[154] The roommate was told this information during the weekend of April 5—6, 2013, while Brandon and the roommate were back in St. Louis. If Brandon had left the Mission church before April of 2013, it is unclear as to where he was employed.

Real Life Church

Brandon again was on the move in August of 2013. He was hired by the Real Life Church[155] in Valencia, California. This would be Brandon's last place of residency until his arrest in St. Louis on February 7, 2014. Two days before Brandon was arrested, he tweeted this comment: "Who I am hates who I've been,"[156] a reference to a song by the group, Relient K. Full lyrics to the song are available via the band's Youtube channel:

https://www.youtube.com/watch?v=8HeuMiuj_Sg

The Allegations 2

The Revelation
Shortly after Brandon left FCCF in January of 2012, the senior pastor[157] at FCCF had received a call from the minister at Gateway Christian Church about a rumored concern involving Brandon, a mother and a student connected to FCCF. The mother was concerned about the amount of time Brandon was spending with her teenage son. The minister at Gateway had heard about the rumored concern from a student attending SLCC. He had heard about the concern from a youth sponsor at FCCF, Dawn Varvil.

---

[154] Phone interview with the former roommate on March 4, 2015.

[155] Real Life Church, http://www.reallifechurch.org/.

[156] Written by Matt Thiessen, lead singer for Reliant K

It was from a song by Reliant K, Twitter, February 5, 2012, https://twitter.com/brandoburn/status/431219890561617920

[157] He is still the current senior minister.

The senior pastor at FCCF and the executive minister[158]invited Dawn Varvil to come to the senior minister's office to respond to these rumors. Dawn met with the two pastors from FCCF for over two hours. Immediately afterwards, Dawn stopped by my house, very distraught and obviously shaken. Over the next several hours, Dawn shared with me and then with my wife, Tamara, a long list of disturbing alleged sexual allegations between Brandon and a group of boys, all minors, from the youth group at FCCF. These alleged allegations took place between 2009 and 2012.

Up to this point, I did not have any strong suspicions or any credible evidence of any inappropriate sexual or emotional relationships with minors by Brandon, nor had I ever been told of any complaints or allegations from any students from the college; any youth, parent, or staff from the church; or any individual outside of the church — no one — until February of 2012.

Here is a list of key alleged allegations Dawn reported to the senior minister and the executive minister in February of 2012 and then shared with me and my wife in our home:

1. Brandon had a male minor staying with him — off and on — in an apartment located across the street from McCluer North High School. Brandon was employed at the church and later was a youth volunteer at the church during these episodes. Brandon gave the minor a key to his apartment and gave him gifts, including an iPad and an iPhone. The iPhone was included on Brandon's cell phone contract and was purchased specifically for the minor.

2. Before Brandon moved to the apartment, he had lived with the parent from FCCF. On more than one occasion, the parent witnessed Brandon in the same sofa bed as the minor, sleeping in a "spooning" position.

3. After the parent shared this information with a counselor, the counselor hot lined Brandon to the proper authorities. Although the counselor was told there was not enough evidence to warrant a further investigation, the counselor was obligated as a mandatory reporter.

---

[158] He is no longer employed at FCCF.

4. The parent contacted the mother of the minor and informed her of the following facts: a) Brandon had given both an iPad and an iPhone to the minor, b) Brandon had included the minor on his cell phone plan, c) Brandon had given a key to his apartment to the minor, d) Brandon frequently allowed the minor to spend the night at the apartment alone with Brandon.

5. The parent, after conferring with another pastor, hot lined Brandon for a second time. Again, although there was not enough evidence to investigate, the parent was told it was important to demonstrate a pattern of inappropriate behavior.

6. Brandon contacted this parent and asked to meet alone with the parent. Brandon and the parent met at a park in Florissant. Upon arrival Brandon expressed to the parent his relief that the parent had come without the police. Brandon then talked about his "emotional" relationship with the minor, pleading with the parent to convince the minor to return to him because the minor's mother had cut off her son's relationship with Brandon.

7. Five males from the church, all minors, told the parent's minor daughter, that Brandon had exposed himself to the boys and had convinced them to expose themselves to Brandon.

The above key alleged allegations were part of the first edition of this case study I had sent to the elders (including Steve Wingfield) on March 3, 2015. I am now[159] including more specific notes of the meeting. Dawn says this is a summary of a meeting with Steve Wingfield and Scott Strandell in Steve Wingfield's office in February 2012 with her. This information is what Dawn shared with me when she visited me in my home after her meeting with Steve and Scott.

Information I shared with Steve and Scott

1. I had contacted the mother of a male minor by phone earlier in the week to make her aware of some concerning facts regarding her minor son and his relationship with Brandon Milburn.

---

[159] March 28, 2015.

a. Her son had been given a key to Brandon's apartment, which was only a few blocks from his home and directly across the street from the minor's school.

b. I had been told by another student that the minor had been telling his mother that he was staying overnight in my home when, in fact, he had been staying the night in Brandon's apartment.

c. I had not seen or heard from the minor in quite some time, and that if he had been telling her that he was spending time at my house, he was lying.

d. Brandon had included her minor son on his cell phone plan and purchased an iPhone for him as a gift.

e. Brandon had gifted her minor son an iPad.

2. Virgil Brazle had contacted me by phone the same day that I had spoken to the minor's mother, and he berated me for contacting her. He then told me that he would not allow me to be a youth sponsor at FCCF because I was "harassing" one of the other youth sponsors (referring to Brandon Milburn). Virgil then argued the validity of my concerns and whether or not it was appropriate to contact the mother with those concerns.

3. Prior to Brandon getting his own apartment, he had been living with my family. During that time, Brandon and I had many conversations about appropriate boundaries with the teen boys, particularly sleeping in bed with them.

4. I had personally witnessed Brandon sleeping in a spooning position with his arms wrapped around the above-mentioned minor.

5. That my daughter Chelsea had shared with me that a group of her male friends had told her that Brandon had exposed his genitals to them and that they had exposed their genitals to him at his request.

6. That I had confronted Brandon about the alleged exposure, and that he had minimized it and explained away as being just playful stuff that guys do.

7. I had discussed the above concerns about Brandon with my counselor.

8. My counselor had called and reported Brandon to Department of Family Services for the above-mentioned concerns.

9. I had discussed the above concerns with my mentor Lisa Womble.

10. I had called the Department of Family Services and reported the above-mentioned concerns at the suggestion of my mentor.

11. I had discussed with Brandon the necessity of him speaking with a counselor regarding his relationship with the above referenced minor.

12. I had provided Brandon with the name and phone number of a qualified counselor.

13. Brandon had told me that he had set an appointment with him but that I was unsure if he had kept the appointment.

14. How difficult it had been for me to carry out all of the above because of the close personal relationship Brandon had shared with my family. That I cared deeply for not only the minor child and his health and well-being but also for the health and well-being of Brandon as a brother in Christ.

Feedback I received from Steve

1. He told me that he had received a phone call from the pastor at Gateway Christian Church saying that someone had come to him with concerns about Brandon Milburn being sexually inappropriate with minors because I had told a student at SLCC that he had been inappropriate with one of my sons. (To which I replied surprise because I had NOT relayed to the student that he was not being inappropriate with one of my sons).

2. He asked if any of my natural children had been abused (To which I replied "no").

3. He told me that if he believed that any child had been mistreated that he would be willing to hotline.

4. He said something to the effect that his son Joshua was also an artist and that sometimes people misunderstand artistic, talented people and mislabeled them as gay. He in effect told me that Brandon Milburn was no more gay than his own son.

5. He stated that if he believed Brandon was capable of things we had discussed that he never would have recommended Brandon to his son-in-law who Brandon had been working with at Gateway Christian Church.

6. He stated that even in light of the information I had given him, he would have no misgivings in recommending Brandon to other churches and would readily write a letter of recommendation for him (paraphrased).

7. He questioned my ability to objectively assess the situation with Brandon, questioned my emotional state and suggested that I take care of my family and distance myself from the situation with Brandon.

8. He stated that he would "Stake his career" on Brandon's innocence.

Feedback I received from Scott

1. Scott told me that he wanted to make it clear to me that Brandon's contract with FCCF had not been renewed in January because he had not carried out all of his job duties properly and stressed to me that it was "for no other reason."

2. Scott stated that Brandon had been very close to his own family and that he cared for him as a son. He continued on that he had had conversations in the past with Brandon regarding appropriate boundaries with students and that he would continue to.

This was the first time I had heard from a reliable source about any alleged allegations of sexual contact by Brandon with minors from the church.

If they were true, I was grieved—grieved for the pain placed upon these innocent and trusting minors, grieved for the impact this would have on the church, and grieved that such a talented and gifted young man could be involved in such despicable acts.

Yet I was not completely surprised—I was beginning to connect the dots.

The Rejection

I was equally grieved and shocked at what I heard next. Concerning these alleged allegations, Dawn said[160] that the senior minister commented that he would stake his career on Brandon's innocence. He said that he would not have written a letter of recommendation to Gateway if he had believed he was guilty of improper sexual activity. The senior minister was a supporter of Brandon.

Since then, I have learned that the minister at Gateway reported that the senior minister at FCCF did not inform him about any of these alleged allegations during the entire time of Brandon's employment at Gateway.[161]

Also, a former college roommate and a former worship leader and intern at FCCF, who had worked with Brandon[162], reinforced this sentiment. He[163] states the senior minister was "in his own words, a 'kindred spirit-hood' with Brandon." The former intern also says that the senior minister

> "was vocal in his admiration for Brandon's creativity, his commitment to ministering to students, and for Brandon as a friend, on a personal level. (He) thought Brandon was cool, charismatic and extremely talented. This was clear by how (the senior minister) talked about Brandon but was probably more apparent by (the senior minister's) actions."

---

[160] The description of the meeting is from the perspective of only the parent. The senior minister and the executive minister have been asked repeatedly to present their perspectives of this meeting, but they have, as of the present, ignored any requests.

[161] Phone interview with the senior minister at Gateway on March 3, 2015.

[162] He worked with Brandon from August of 2009 to May of 2011.

[163] From a phone conversation on March 4, 2015 and an Email from March 5, 2015.

"Brandon would move back and forth between Florissant and Louisville, Kentucky or California, and upon his return each time, the senior minister would offer him a higher position with more responsibility than the job he had previously. No other intern or staff member received the same treatment."

"Further, the senior minster openly considered Brandon 'like-minded' with himself and it seemed to me that he would give Brandon the benefit of the doubt in any situation. In short, the senior minister admired, favored, and just plain liked Brandon as a person and as a minister."

Near the end of the meeting, Dawn stated the senior minister began to question her own mental capacity to the point that when she arrived at my house, she began to question the severity of the allegations. My wife and I, however, immediately reassured Dawn that these alleged allegations were very serious and that she had acted legally and morally by reporting them to the two pastors.

These alleged allegations — shared by a key church member whose children knew the very boys with whom Brandon hung out — should have been enough to warrant a church-wide investigation.

These alleged allegations — reported by a youth sponsor who spent extensive time ministering to the very boys with whom Brandon was accused of abusing — should have been enough to call for an examination of the charges.

These alleged allegations — conveyed by a parent who had the courage and strength to bring them to light — should have been enough to launch a probe into the alleged allegations.

It should have been enough — but it was not enough!

The Consultation

My wife and I laid out three imperatives concerning these alleged allegations. Dawn had already carried out two of them; I was about to carry out the third one.

1. Brandon had to be hot lined to the proper authorities — the parent and her counselor had each fulfilled this one.

2. The alleged allegations had to be reported to the church leadership — the parent had just warned the senior and executive ministers.

3. Brandon had to be confronted about the alleged allegations — I would follow through with this one about a week later.

When I asked Brandon, in my office at the college, about each of the alleged allegations, he blew off the one alleged allegation of exposing himself to the five minors by saying, "it was just something boys do when they are joking around." Brandon denied any inappropriate behavior with the minor staying at his apartment. In fact, he denied any type of inappropriate sexual behavior with any individuals at the church. He looked away from me often, staring down at the floor. He was not shocked or intimidated by his questions — it was as if he had already been prepared for them. As he walked out of my office, Brandon would cut off our six-and-a-half-year friendship, not wanting to have any contact with me during the remaining time he volunteered at FCCF, including teaching at Hydrate on Wednesday evenings.

But I now knew, for the first time, that Brandon was most likely involved in some type of inappropriate sexual activity with young boys. Although there wasn't enough objective evidence to warrant an arrest, there was enough circumstantial evidence to begin to connect the dots to be highly suspicious of Brandon. It was then that I began my own investigation by putting together a narrative of Brandon's story, documenting his history at the college and at the church — thus the genesis of this story.[164]

The Request

About a month after these alleged allegations were shared with the two pastors, Dawn sent me a text from Brandon.[165] By this time, the minor's mother had requested her son to cut off his relationship with Brandon.

---

[164] Looking back on the story, I would have informed the senior and executive ministers that the parent had informed me about the allegations, and I would have informed the minister at Gateway about them also. I did not hotline Brandon after I talked to him because he had already been hotlined twice for the same allegations. The lesson learned about sexual abuse allegations—report.

[165] Text message from Brandon to the parent on March 18, 2012.

So Brandon sent Dawn this text, begging Dawn to convince the mother to let her son, under the age of 16, to return to Brandon. The names of the people in the text have been replaced with their titles, and no revisions of the original text have been made.

"So, I've been going back and forth on whether or not i should send this text. But i just have to. Its' similar to that "momma bear" feeling you always told me about. And i get it. totally now.

I see (The Minor) as my son and God had definitely been guiding that so similar to Paul and Timothy and Jesus and John. We were closer and closer. And now I have this feeling that I would do anything to get my son back. This text is not to accuse you of anything but to just tell you what has happened. (The Minor) has no phone anymore (not a big deal) but (The Minor) can never see me ever again, he isn't allowed any communication with me. and worst of all he can't attend church anymore.

His parents told me how they were surprised I was fired from fccf for accusations against me regarding teen boys. But the reality is, they have no idea that their son went from Saul to Paul. that he's been clean of drugs and alcohol for a year and a half, that he's remained sexual pure. And not to have an ego boost there, but it was because of how I guided (The Minor). They see me as a bad person and a threat to their son, when in reality I was the very vessel that God used to help same him. (The Minor) messed up by keeping of our activities from them. I know that. What I do know is that (The Minor) stopped lying about going to your house a while back. And he didn't lie about going to (Name) or (Name)...he just never updated them after he was with those guys.

My request is simple please, please, please, please call his mom back today and let her know how good I was/am for (The Minor). Please let her know his past before I came into his life. And please let her know that the only reason he hid the relationship from her was because he was used to hiding things from her before and that I urged him to tell her things. And he started to.

I am willing to jump through any hoop, pay any amount, go anywhere, do anything, I will do whatever you want, because what God had been doing in that boys' life the past 4 weeks was incredible. He was planning to ask his mom about going on a mission trip (without me) and had started preaching to his friends on Facebook. He even talked about attending bible college. We read the bible together every night. he started showing signs of mentoring younger boys on simple levels. He is a good kid who made a simple mistake. And now he's facing persecution. I was filled with bitterness and rage and anger, and I let it all pass. But what remains is a heart for a son. To continue to raise him up in the LORD. please call her today. please"

Dawn did not, at any time, ask the mother to let her son return to Brandon. But it was still during this time that Brandon was volunteering at FCCF on Wednesday evenings.

A current youth sponsor at FCCF who served as a leader during FCCF's late night Sunday evening service from February to May of 2012 came forward recently and reported to me:

> During this time, I would regularly see Brandon Milburn at these services, often coming in during the middle of the service, and always accompanied by teens. I knew Brandon was no longer on staff at the time, but did not question his presence, seeing it at the time as him just being a good mentor to students he had been guiding during his time at Florissant. What would often make me tilt my head and question was that every time Brandon was there, he would always have his arm around a student. It was nothing that gave me any suspicion of inappropriate behavior, just something that I felt was rather odd.[166]

This youth sponsor added that during most of these Sunday evening services from February to May of 2012, the senior minister preached at these services, and that he would have witnessed Brandon attending the services accompanied by minors.

---

[166] Facebook message from the youth sponsor on March 26, 2015.

This occurred after the senior minister had been made aware of the alleged allegations from February of 2012 by Dawn Varvil!

The Arrest 3

A few days before Brandon's arrest, a detective appeared at the Dawn's home because Brandon had listed Dawn's address as his St. Louis residence. Dawn was informed that Brandon was going to be arrested when he arrived in St. Louis. A day after his arrest, Dawn called me — Brandon was in police custody.

That evening, February 8, 2014, I phoned Titus to share the news of Brandon's arrest.

The day before the news[167] broke on all of the media outlets in St. Louis, I visited[168] Brandon at the Saint Louis County jail. He appeared dazed and confused, quite surprised to see me. On my second visit a week later, Brandon told me to not tell anyone he was in jail; it was too late — his mug shot had been plastered all over the media. His secret was out. When the story did break in St. Louis, FCCF released this statement to the press on February 11, 2014 by the Executive Minister[169]:

> "Having just heard of these charges from something that happened in 2007, our first concern is with how we can best help any victim heal, 'The charges point to a time when as a college student he served in a part time role as an intern. For the last several years he has been living in another state. We have a justice system who can do the investigation and we will assist them any way we can as our church family works through this.'"[170]

---

[167] Fox 2 News Saint Louis http://fox2now.com/2014/02/11/youth-minister-arrested-for-sexually-assaulting-children/

[168] February 10, 2014. The news broke on TV on February 11, 2014.

[169] He was not the same executive minister from 2012 that met with the senior minister and Dawn about the alleged allegations. This executive minister was hired after Feb of 2012. It is not known if he was told about the alleged allegations by the senior minister.

[170] St. Louis Post-Dispatchhttp://www.stltoday.com/news/local/crime-and-courts/california-youth-minister-faces-sodomy-charges-in-st-louis-county/article_3d3299f1-cd97-56d4-baf9-d63e5572efe6.html

When the executive minister[171] was asked later about why the press release did not fit with the time-line of Brandon's time at FCCF, he said, "I can say with 100% certainty I communicated the exact information I received."[172]

The senior minister then addressed the charges against Brandon during one Sunday morning service. He then communicated the church's concern with a number of small groups during one Wednesday night event at the church building. His address is presented below in its entirety:

> This past week has been difficult as news reported on the arrest regarding a very serious crime. For the next five minutes I need to lead us in a family talk as a dad myself with two teenagers and as your pastor. Sometimes in the very best families, bad things happen. If you don't know already, it was revealed this past week that someone was arrested. He was arrested a week ago Friday, for hurting a couple of kids. The person charged is Brandon Milburn. He moved away two years ago but during a time between 2007 and 2009 he allegedly sexually abused two eleven-year old boys. This while he was a college student and working here part-time as an intern. And it made our local news on Tuesday. I think I know how many of you feel. That makes me both angry and sad all at the same time. Because we want this to be a safe place for you, for your children, just like I would for my daughters.
>
> How many of you are parents in this room? As parents, I want you to know Wednesday night I had a difficult task of speaking to a group of about 130, 150 teenagers on Wednesday night. And I need you to know what I told them. I told them two things—a hard truth and what we can do about it. The hard truth is sometimes people we trust may try to touch us or get us to do something that is wrong. That's a hard truth. And the thing we do about it is if anyone ever makes you feel uncomfortable or unsafe, young people, we want you to tell your parents, your school counselor, tell a pastor, even if it's embarrassing to talk about it. Parent, a school counselor, a pastor will listen and help.

---

[171] He is not the executive minister who heard the allegations in 2012. He was hired after that event.

[172] Executive Minister: Email from March 15, 2015.

And then I had to work my way around to six or seven different small groups that meet here in the church, and I had to say to parents that were here, you need to know what I told your teenagers, but it's not my job, it's not the church's job, to give explicit definitions of sex crimes to young children in mix settings like at a local church or in a public setting. That's a parent's responsibility.

So, we encourage all parents to talk to their children and look them in the eye and say if ever anything happens that makes you feel embarrassed, or if it makes you feel uncomfortable or unsafe you can tell me. I want you to tell me. You can tell your school counselor, you can tell your pastor, and I will listen and I will always love you.

You know no matter what happened in the past not every case makes the news or gets reported. And I looked up the statistics from an accurate source, the National Center for the Victims of Crime based out of Washington DC, and one out of five girls and one out of ten boys are sexually abused in our country. So, if you have been hurt by something like this, you need to know you are not alone and the good news is that you can get past this, and you can heal in this place. We know a healer and he can heal anybody of anything, amen?

Listen, we are not a perfect church, I am very imperfect as a pastor, our leaders are imperfect, and you at times, you're not all that either. But our desire is to be people of truth and holiness and to help people to heal through the life changing power of the good news that we have to share. You know one of Satan's oldest ploys is to create distractions for the church from its core mission to connect people to Jesus, and I am glad as a church family we're not going to let something bad that happened years ago keep us from doing good right now and as a church family we are going to stay positive. We are going to keep preaching Jesus. We are going to help people heal cause that's what we do here. That's what's this family is all about. Amen.[173]

---

[173] Steve Wingfield's address to FCCF concerning the arrest of Brandon Milburn on February 16, 2014 at the FCCF worship service, https://vimeo.com/87521576 Time 25:49-31:15.

Surely these two pro-active actions were enough to finally jump-start the investigation into the alleged allegations from 2012. I had assumed that during the eleven months leading up to the trial, the elders of FCCF had investigated the alleged allegations, first by interviewing this parent and second, by interviewing others, including myself.

I was, however, shocked and dumbfounded to discover that no staff or elder had ever followed-up with the parent concerning these alleged allegations!

In fact, a former staff member reported that at the time of the arrest he was surprised. He said,

> "I can verify that what was communicated to the staff when the arrest happened was that leadership was completely shocked by the news and they had never been made aware before of any inappropriate behavior."[174]

Another former staff member echoed this same surprise about any allegations,

> "What you wrote explained to me what some were posting on Facebook right after his arrest about something being known before.
> As far as I knew this was the first that anybody knew about accusations."[175]

Shouldn't the arrest have been enough to convince the leadership of FCCF to investigate the 2012 alleged allegations? Shouldn't the six counts of sodomy that had occurred nearly 7 years previously have been enough to move the leadership to reexamine the parent's warnings? Shouldn't the $100,000 cash-only bond have been enough to show the seriousness of the charges to wake-up the leadership to reconsider the alleged allegations from 2012?

It should have been enough — but it was not enough!

---

[174] Facebook Message March 17, 2015.

[175] Facebook Message March 16, 2015.

After the charges were released to the public, I assumed the two victims were boys from the 2012 alleged allegations. It was eight months later, however, when I learned the shocking news — these two victims were not connected to the alleged allegations of 2012.

A Time to Act

It was enough for me to act.

My wife and I met with the family of one of the victims who had come forward. I talked with a family member of the other victim. I contacted the Saint Louis County prosecuting attorney, sharing with him the 2012 alleged allegations first reported to the leadership at FCCF and sharing the church's failure to follow-up on them with this parent. As the trial date of January 26, 2015 approached, the prosecuting attorney subpoenaed Titus and me as potential witnesses. I revised and wrote several more drafts of this story in preparation for a trial. Fortunately for the highly vulnerable victims, they did not have to testify publicly.

Without any fanfare or media blitz, Brandon Milburn pleaded guilty to not six, but seven counts of sodomy with two minors under the age of 12 on a Monday morning at the Saint Louis County courthouse on January 26, 2015. He still awaits sentencing as of March 30, facing a prison term from 10 years to life.

So ends the story of Brandon Milburn, for the victims and their families, the college, and the church — or does it?

The Plan 4

Called to Lead

This is simply the middle of the story, a story that is not completed, a story that is not finished, a story that continues to be written.

Since the guilty plea, I have become aware of two more alleged allegations[176] of sexual abuse with minors by Brandon — raising the number of alleged victims by Brandon to eight, not including the two victims from 2007.

---

[176] Interview in February of 2015 with a former FCCF youth sponsor and parent.

The consequences and fall-out from Brandon Milburn's actions at FCCF and potentially other churches will not simply go away when Brandon goes away to prison in a few weeks. FCCF is not ready to "move on" and "put this behind them" as much as they might want to. FCCF must slow down, FCCF must investigate the fall-out, FCCF must learn from this tragedy, and FCCF must prepare to bring healing, comfort, and justice to any and all of the people affected, directly or indirectly, by the actions of one young man — Brandon.

The elders must lead this call; they are called to be the leaders.

Over thirty years ago, I was ordained to the ministry. I have had the honor and privilege to serve the church in multiple positions as a youth minister, co-pastor, missionary, senior minister, elder; in different locations overseas and in the states; and in a variety of environments with well-established churches and new church plants.

I understand that the biblical role of a pastor / elder, carries with it a high privilege:

"If anyone aspires to the office of overseer, he desires a noble task.[177]

The role of a pastor/elder also brings with it a tremendous responsibility to —

> "shepherd the flock of God that is among you, exercising oversight, not under compulsion, but willingly, as God would have you; not for shameful gain, but eagerly; not domineering over those in your charge, but being examples to the flock. And when the chief Shepherd appears, you will receive the unfading crown of glory."[178]

The elders must shepherd the flock, a flock of confused and hurting young boys affected by these events, a flock of angry and frustrated parents trying to make sense of this, a flock of volunteers and workers attempting to figure out how they missed all of the signs, and a flock of leaders feeling overwhelmed with how to manage these events.

---

[177] 1 Timothy 3:1 ESV

[178] 1 Peter 5:1–4 ESV

Initiate an Investigation

To begin this process of implementing a plan, Titus sent an initial letter to the elders at FCCF on February 27, 2015, laying out the need for the elders to initiate an investigation. The letter has been printed below in its entirety:

Dear Elders of First Christian,

As you are all aware, Brandon Milburn was arrested one year ago on charges of sodomy. These charges eventually resulted in a guilty plea. His punishment will be severe, and rightly so. Throughout this process, I have cooperated with the prosecuting attorney in the case. I was set to serve as a witness had the case gone to trial. Fortunately for the victims it did not come to that. As sentencing draws near, I wanted to take a chance to reach out to each of you.

In the past year, I have become aware of many details regarding this case. I've done my best to handle that information with care, including consulting legal advice and maintaining communication with the Prosecuting Attorney's office.

Among the disturbing information I've been made aware of is the fact that Steve Wingfield and Scott Strandell spoke in early 2012 with someone expressing great concern regarding an inappropriate relationship between Brandon and a male student. My understanding is that specific examples were cited to communicate the severity of these concerns, yet the church did not act on this information.

More troubling, it seems the church has attempted to distance themselves as much from this situation as possible, including:

- Steve assuring people that prior to Brandon's arrest he had no knowledge of abuse allegations, which is false, as concerns were shared with him in 2012.

- Failing to reach out to the victims or their families despite expressing this as a "first Priority" to the congregation and public.

- Failing to attempt to reach out to possible additional victims.

- Failing to alert churches where Brandon subsequently served, both in MO and CA.

In the last twelve months, I have done a disproportionate amount of pastoral work with people on all sides of this issue. Doing this from 900 miles away is a challenge and should not be necessary, but I am willing to do what I can to facilitate healing. However, it seems there has been a leadership vacuum from the church. Frankly, I believe the church has failed to handle this situation correctly, both in 2012 after concerns were voiced to Steve and Scott as well as since Brandon's arrest. Not proactively pastoring victims, potential victims and many other individuals who are hurting over this situation are all examples of this failure. Distancing yourself may be the safe thing to do, but it is morally wrong and a failure of Steve's and the rest of the elder's leadership. It was also against the law.

I have been in contact with additional victims and helped to coordinate their interaction with legal authorities and counseling resources. I have fielded countless phone calls from concerned parents. I have ministered directly to the victim's families. I have given advice to people wondering how they might communicate with and minister to Brandon. I have been in ongoing communication with the prosecuting attorney. I've talked to churches where Brandon served after he left Florissant. That First Christian has not led in this effort is outrageous.

I have given the church a year to coordinate conversations and publicly lead the faith community in appropriate ways. There is so much that has happened that remains a secret, and that is not acceptable. There are people who are suffering and — because of the church's perceived silence — look at the church as a co-conspirator instead of an agency of healing. This is also unacceptable.

I am watching hopefully to see the church right some of its wrongs; however, I'm not waiting any longer to assist in making these things right. I will cooperate with any attempt to shine light on the failures of the past. I am beyond frustrated at the way this has been managed and heartbroken that the church I once called home and love deeply has mishandled this situation so severely. By failing to report allegations in 2012, failing to follow up with known victims, seek out other victims, and being disingenuous with the facts (with multiple people and news outlets), First Christian has invited suspicion. That suspicion may be unwarranted, but it does exist.

Giving people the opportunity to know the truth, talk about what happened, and move on healthily is my goal. It is particularly true that I want this for the victims who were ignored in 2012 when the church became aware of alleged abuse against them. I am coming to you as directly as I can with all of this out of respect of the office of the elders as well as out of respect for each of you as individuals. I count you as brothers in the faith.

I worked with Brandon as closely as anyone. I never suspected a thing. I have great regrets over that fact. However, my greatest regret is that no one ever came to me with the suspicious behaviors they observed or concerns about alleged abuse. Had they, I most certainly would've acted. Why didn't you guys do more? Ongoing abuse as Brandon volunteered in 2012 or victims in California — if there are any — most certainly could've been avoided by more decisive action.

Ultimately what I am asking for is some public recognition of these failures as well as accountability for and corrections to the insufficient response. For Steve and Scott and any alerted staff members for not adequately handling concerns raised about Brandon in 2012 as well as the rest of the elders for failing to insist on greater pastoral care for the many people who have been so deeply affected by all this. Please take steps to make this right.

Don't hesitate to contact me if you have any questions.

Sincerely, Titus Benton

Following Titus's letter to all of the elders, I sent the first edition of this document on March 3, including the following three-fold Strategy for the Elders, to begin the conversation, to begin the healing, to continue the story.

A Three-Fold Strategy

1. The story is unfinished — the elders must minister to all the victims, to their families, and to any church members affected by this event. The elders should:

   - Apologize, support, and applaud the two victims, who with great courage and strength of character, came forward without the support of the church, to stop Brandon from hurting more young boys.

   - Surround the families of the victims with love and support, apologizing for ignoring their pain and praying for their recovery.

   - Reach out and care for any of the volunteers, youth sponsors, and parents who were affected by Brandon's actions.

   - Apologize to Dawn Varvil for ignoring her allegations from three years ago and for minimizing her motives.

   - Work tirelessly to identify, assess, support, and care for the needs of any other victims — those included in the alleged allegations of 2012 and any new allegations — for as long as it takes to bring healing and restoration to them in the name of Christ.

   - Pray for confession and repentance for Brandon and for restoration and reconciliation with the church as he enters into the prison system, remembering Jesus' words to visit those in prison.

2. The story is unfinished — the elders must reexamine the church's official statement released to the press on February 11, 2014. The elders should:

   - Recognize that the official statement released to the press was incorrect. Brandon had not been living in California the past "several years" but had actually been working at Gateway Christian Church and volunteering in the Wednesday evening youth program between February and May of 2012.

- Investigate why the official statement was inaccurate and released to the press.

3. The story is unfinished—the elders must initiate an extensive investigation into any mismanagement or failures by the senior pastor/ elders/ or staff in handling this situation and thoroughly reassess all of the church's policies and procedures concerning sexual abuse allegations. The elders should:

- Investigate any past or current alleged allegations immediately. Although Brandon was brought to justice, the legal authorities will not investigate any other alleged charges nor interview any potential victims unless they come forward first. Until they do, the church cannot hide behind the law and not conduct its own internal investigation of past or current alleged allegations.

- Consider the example of the Real Life Church in Santa Clara, California, who although they had received no complaints about Milburn, they still opened an internal investigation on February 13, 2014, only days after his arrest.[179]The church posted that "the church is reaching out to members through email, Facebook and meetings to try to communicate what the church knows, Gray said, although officials at Real Life Church are still conducting their own investigation into the situation." [180]

  They also stated, "Milburn, who worked with the church for about five and a half months, came highly recommended by references, including a pastor in St. Louis, Gray said. Church officials have been "horrified" by the accusations, he said."[181]

---

[179] SIGNALscv.com http://www.signalscv.com/archives/114294/

[180] KHTS AM 1220 http://www.hometownstation.com/santa-clarita-news/crime/real-life-church-pastor-addresses-concern-over-former-employee-40396

[181] KHTS AM 1220http://www.hometownstation.com/santa-clarita-news/crime/real-life-church-pastor-addresses-concern-over-former-employee-40396

Remember that Brandon had been associated with FCCF, not for 5½ months but for nearly 5½ years, and that FCCF had received complaints—by a youth sponsor / parent—of alleged allegations of sexual behavior against not one but numerous minors from the church.

- Ask a series of questions of all church staff, elders, deacons, volunteers, teachers, and members who may have had a role, directly or indirectly, in Brandon's nearly 5½ years at FCCF, and when necessary, take corrective action.

  1. Was Brandon hot lined to the authorities by the senior and executive ministers as mandatory reporters? If not, why not?

  2. Was Gateway Christian Church made known of these alleged allegations after Brandon left his employment at FCCF?[182] If not, why not?

  3. Were staff and/or elders at FCCF made aware of the allegations in 2012? If so, to whom and when? If not, why?

  4. Was either of the two churches in California given letters of recommendation from the senior minister? If so, what were the recommendations?

  5. Were the three churches in California made aware of these allegations? If not, why not?

  6. Did the staff and/or elders do a follow-up investigation with the parent who brought the allegations to the senior and executive ministers? If so, when and how? If not, why not?

  7. Why did Brandon continue to be a youth volunteer on Wednesday nights during the spring of 2012 after the revelation of the allegations were made known?

  8. Have any staff and/or elders met with the two victims and their families to provide pastoral and spiritual support? If not, why not?

---

[182] Since the initial edition of this story on March 3, 2015, it has been revealed that Gateway Christian Church was not made aware of these alleged allegations.

9. Have the staff and/or elders met with Brandon while he is in the Saint Louis County jail? If so, who and why? If not, why not?

10. Have any staff/elders/deacons/teachers been contacted by anyone, inside or outside the church, with any information, concerns or suspensions related to Brandon's behavior with minors? If so, who and when? What was done with the information?

11. Have any staff/elders/deacons/teachers initiated any communications with anyone, inside and outside the church, concerning any information, concerns, or suspicions related to Brandon's inappropriate behavior with minors? If so, who, when, and why?

- Examine, assess, and revise problems with the church's policies and procedures concerning any type of abusive, ungodly, or illegal behavior — physical, sexual, or emotional — displayed by any staff or member of FCCF.

- Reassure the congregation that the leadership is committed to protecting the church, particularly the most vulnerable members — its youth — from predators and promise to take any and all future complaints or allegations of sexual abuse seriously.

- Pray for wisdom and discernment, practice confession and repentance, and seek forgiveness and reconciliation.

The Response 5

The Certified Letter

On March 19, 2015, Titus and I received a reply from the elders, a certified letter — with no names — in response to this document. It is reprinted below in its entirety:

March 17, 2015

Douglas Lay
2409 Lavin Court
Florissant, MO 63033

Dear Mr. Lay

It is clear that you care deeply about this tragic situation. The actions of one have hurt many, including you. As well, our whole church family has been a victim of this sin and violation of trust.

While we have and will continue to cooperate fully with the legal process, it is not appropriate for us to discuss this with you.[183] We have a culture of zero tolerance of child abuse and remain committed to making safety of children our highest priority.

We are thankful that two victims came forward so that the authorities could conduct an open investigation and seek a judgment. As part of our complete cooperation with the instructions of the prosecuting attorney, as a church we have not taken the role of investigator.[184]

In each public announcement we encouraged other victims, if any, to communicate directly with those handling the case. We believe honoring victims includes allowing them to initiate communication and process healing through the counselors of their choosing.[185]

---

[183] It is unclear as to why the elders believe it is not appropriate to discuss this with me. I have reached out to them on five occasions, asking them to, as in the words of one of the current staff members, "fill in the gaps." So, I will continue to send the elders requests for their perspective.

[184] This is unclear. Why not? The prosecuting attorney does not prohibit a church from doing its own investigation; in fact, he would welcome it. The Real Church in CA conducted its own investigation after the arrest of Brandon in 2014.

[185] This clearly displays ignorance about how to minister to alleged victims. They almost never will come forward on their own without the proactive initiative, in this case, of the church. This is simply a smoke screen to avoid any legal liability.

As we have reviewed your correspondence, we feel that it contains a number of inaccuracies and does not fairly or accurately describe communications with our church or our approach.[186] It is our desire though not to add to speculation or discord in forums such a social media as this has great potential for adding hurt to victims.[187]

We have confidence in the expertise of the law enforcement personnel. We will continue to defer to their investigation and prosecution of Brandon Milburn.[188] The sentencing will likely involve sever penalties. As we did last year, we expect to provide additional training of our servant leaders to be alert to abuse and to help assure persons who may be victims that they should not feel personal shame for the actions of another.

It is our prayerful hope that through this process the victims, their families, and others affected by this tragedy will attain justice and healing. As for this ministry, our determination is to move forward sharing the good news of the powerful and healing name of Jesus Christ.

In Christ's Service

Elders, First Christian

Titus contacted the Prosecuting Attorney's office handling Brandon Milburn's case shortly after receiving this letter.

---

[186] I have asked the elders on five occasions to correct, altar, add, or deny any of the information in this document, yet they choose to remain silent. It is totally disingenuous to declare a number of inaccuracies exist and then in the same breath declare their refusal to address them. They may send any corrections to **isitenough15@gmail.com**.

[187] I did not request the elders to address the content of this document in social media; I requested they address them in only private correspondences, by email or in person, with me. The issue at hand is how the elders have dealt with the alleged victims.

[188] Their letter addressed the current two victims only for which Brandon has already pleaded guilty. This document addresses the elders' failure to address the alleged allegations of six other alleged victims. There is no legal investigation to defer to by the PA against Brandon for these six alleged allegations because the PA's office doesn't investigate alleged victims unless they come forward. But that in no way prevents or hinders the church from assisting in conducting its own investigation. The church's refusal to investigate these alleged allegations is the very reason for writing this very document!

His office said that no one from the church had contacted him about his instructions to the church and that he would be open to any assistance the church could provide.[189] I sent the 4th edition of Is It Enough? to the Prosecuting Attorney's office immediately after discovering this information.[190] His office contacted me the following day (March 20) to follow-up on the eight alleged victims mentioned in the story—welcoming my own investigation! [191] The elders did not address the thesis of this story—knowledge of the 2012 alleged allegations by the senior and executive ministers—and now the elders together have chosen to remain silent as well.

The Message Letter

I then contacted the former FCCF executive minister after receiving this letter from the elders, asking for his help. I said,

> "As you know, Brandon Milburn, who pleaded guilty of sodomy, is about to be sentenced on March 30, 2015. I have been conducting an investigation into Brandon's behavior at the college, which also runs over to the church. I had been his academic adviser for 4.5 years, a mentor, and a member of the same church he attended, So I have put together a narrative, a timeline of his time from 2005 to 2015.

---

[189] Facebook Message from Titus on March 19, 2015.

[190] March 19, 2015. Email sent to Michael Hayes, Prosecuting Attorney for St. Louis County.

[191] Voice mail from Michal Hayes, the PA of St. Louis County on March 20, 2015.

Part of that timeline includes you. I am writing to you, first, to give you a heads-up on the narrative. I will be glad to send you the narrative, if you wish, through an email address, if you would like to send it to me. I do not know or am interested in the situation around your employment or the reasons for leaving the church. But since you are in the narrative, and out of respect for you, I wanted to let you know in advance about the events that led up to his guilty plea. Also, I wanted to give you a heads-up if there are any other investigations. I have been keeping a record since Feb of 2012 when I first became aware of credible allegations against Brandon. I have interviewed numerous former staff workers with Brandon, former students at the college, youth sponsors, and even the families of the victims. I have a vested interest in this situation. So, you can let me know. My cell is _____ or my email at _____ Thank you."[192]

The executive minister replied later that day: "Hello Doug, Thanks for reaching out to me. This is the first I've heard of this, so yes, I would ask that I be sent a copy of this document. My email address is: _____. Thank you."[193]

I sent him the narrative, "Is It Enough?" on March 5, 2015. I sent him an update of the story on March 18th, asking him to make any changes or comments he believed would correct the story. I did not hear from him. Then after receiving the elders' letter from FCCF, I sent him this message[194]:

> I need your help. I will be straight up with you. Here is the letter from the elders to me about the story, "Is It Enough?" I am going to ask you, for the sake of the other victims, come forward and testify to the conversation the parent had with you and Steve in February of 2012? Please consider it. I need your help. You were there. Don't let this remain silent. Thank you.

---

[192] March 5th, 9:43am
[193] March 5th, 12:06pm
[194] March 19, 2015 at 7:27 pm.

He responded that same day: Doug, I have been advised to not communicate about these accusations.[195]

So, as of March 19, 2015, the situation stood as follows: Concerning the meeting in February of 2012 between Dawn Varvil, the senior minister and the former executive minister about the alleged sexual allegations toward six minors from FCCF, the senior minster is refusing to speak about the meeting, the former executive minister is refusing to speak about the meeting, and none of the current FCCF staff or five elders have ever contacted Dawn Varvil to verify her account of the meeting.

The Open Letter

On Friday evening, March 20, 2015, Kari Benton, the wife of Titus, posted on Facebook an open letter to the senior minister, Steve Wingfield. It is reprinted below in its entirety[196]:

> Dear Steve,
>
> Anyone who knows me well is aware that I hate conflict. I don't like to discuss difficult topics, and especially not publicly. Anyone reading this needs to know that I have written these thoughts down because I felt like I HAD to; because I felt truly convicted to do so. I also need you to know that my motivation in writing is not vindictive or mean-spirited. I have a twenty-year history with the Wingfield family and deeply care for each one of them. Charles sat in my living room when I was just a kid and explained the plan of salvation to my mom and I. Beth was my high school BASICS director. You conducted my uncle's funeral and visited me in the hospital after my son was born.
>
> I am writing publicly to you, Steve, because I have some things that I must say to you and I feel that if I were to do so privately you would ignore or dismiss me, as you have done to others in the recent past. What I want to communicate most clearly is this: You, Steve, are not fit to be lead pastor of the

---

[195] Facebook Message March 19, 2015

[196] Facebook post by Kari Benton on March 20, 2015

First Christian Church of Florissant and you need to turn in your resignation as soon as possible.

This has been my position for many years, but I did not feel the need to speak about it publicly because it mostly affected Titus and me and other staff members. However, recent events have made me decide that I MUST speak up. I know that I am no longer a member at First Christian so you may be tempted to dismiss my words, therefore I'd like to make it clear: Titus resigned from First Christian only because he could no longer work under your poor leadership. If it were not for you, it is very likely we would still be serving at that church today. I care deeply about FCCF and feel an obligation to speak up for those who are unable to speak up for themselves.

Since Brandon Milburn was arrested in February 2014. I have waited for you, Steve, to take strong leadership in helping this faith community to heal from this traumatic reality. Granted, I do not have the knowledge of all that you have said or done in the last year regarding this situation, but I do know that it has not been enough.

Most disturbing is the fact that in 2012 you were made aware by a concerned adult that Brandon was having an inappropriate relationship with a teenage boy and this adult was very confident that Brandon was abusing this boy. Your response to this adult was basically — That's not true, you're crazy for even suggesting that (I'm paraphrasing here). You failed in that moment. Not only should you have believed this concerned adult, but you also should have gotten on the phone and reported these allegations to the authorities. You did neither. After Brandon was arrested you failed again. The first phone call you should have made after learning of his arrest was to that concerned adult that had previously come to you with concerns of abuse. But you did not do that — and to this day you still have not reached out to that concerned adult or to that teenage boy. You have failed both of them.

What makes this even worse is that this is not the first time you have mishandled situations such as these. Many years ago, another young man was found to have inappropriately touched a younger boy. These two situations are not identical, but your responses are eerily similar. In the name of "protecting" this young man you managed to keep this situation from the public. However honorable you might have thought that was, the fact is a victim was silenced at your request. To me, this shows a clear pattern that when something of this nature comes to your attention your initial reaction is to keep it quiet and to do as little possible in order to preserve yours and/or the church's reputation. In considering these two situations, I conclude your actions have proven you to be untrustworthy when it comes to serious circumstances such as abuse. As a result, if another similar situation were to come to your attention in the future, I have absolutely ZERO confidence that you would handle it appropriately. It is unacceptable for a lead pastor to be untrustworthy when it comes to handling serious situations such as abuse.

There are many other ways that you failed to be a suitable leader not only regarding Brandon's situation, but also at many other times throughout the years. You have lied to people about my husband and the reasons he resigned. You have used the pulpit and your sermons to passive aggressively chastise your staff for disagreeing with you. You have stubbornly resisted to listen to members of your congregation that had concerns regarding the turnover of staff members. For all these things I chose not to speak up, but this time is different. This time I am speaking up not for my husband's reputation, but for the victims and the young people who have been hurt and to whom you have failed to effectively minister, which is your job. I know that I have little to gain and much to lose by speaking up like this, but your lack of leadership in this is a much bigger deal than I think you realize. This is not something that can easily be forgotten in a few weeks or months. This is the culmination of a history of consistent leadership failures. For these reasons, the right thing for you to do is to resign.

Will it be difficult? Yes. Will it be painful? Yes. Will the church struggle as a result? Yes. But you are simply not fit for this position—you never were and you still are not. If you truly love the church as much as you claim, you will do what is right and step down.

Kari Benton

Five days[197] following the open letter, the senior minister of FCCF reported to a group of about 30 youth volunteers that he did not know of any allegations against Brandon before his arrest on February of 2014. When asked by a volunteer if a parent had reported to the senior minister any alleged allegations from 2012 (reported to him by Dawn Varvil), the senior minister said there were only "rumors" about the alleged allegations and that the church was not going to investigate the rumors, but rather the church, with the support of the five elders, was going to move ahead. They were not going to talk about Brandon anymore.[198]

The Court Letter

In a few days, Brandon Milburn will appear in the St. Louis County courthouse in Clayton, Missouri, to receive his sentence for seven counts of sodomy against two minors from First Christian Church of Florissant. The judge, who will decide Brandon's sentence, has asked anyone associated with this case to send him a letter as he decides the length of Brandon's incarceration. It is with a heavy heart that I am mailing, Is It Enough? to the judge today.

When the sentencing comes down on March 30, 2015, the judicial system will have completed its role. This case will be over. The legal system will move on. But this story will not be over—it will continue.

The Deacon Letter

On March 25, I sent out the case study, Is It Enough? (5th edition) to nineteen of the deacons at FCCF. One of the deacons responded three days later by sending this letter by email to the elders on Saturday, March 28th. She sent a copy of the letter to me.[199]

---

[197] March 25, 2015. The meeting was at the FCCF facility after a Wednesday evening service. Three individuals lead the meeting: The youth intern, the executive minster, and the senior minister.

[198] Personal interview with two college-age youth sponsors and volunteers on March 26, 2015.

[199] Facebook message received on Saturday, March 28, 2015.

To the Elders:

I'm writing to express deep concern for recent serious and public accusations made against the FCCF leadership. I read the open letter Kari Benton posted on Facebook, and I read the case study on FCCF entitled, "Is it Enough?" by Titus Benton and Professor Doug Lay. I consider all three of these people to be sincere believers who care about honesty and integrity, so their claims disturb me.

There is a piece of the story missing, which is a full disclosure by the church leadership of the events described in these documents. I am a small cog in a huge financial wheel who helps pay salaries for church staff. As I prayerfully come to a decision on what to do with my support in the future, I carefully consider as much information as possible.

As a deacon and a church member, I respectfully request an opportunity to hear your missing account of this issue in an open, honest format before your membership body. I have already been asked about what's going on by some of the members to whom I minister in Celebrate Recovery. I would like them to receive answers to their questions in public on these damaging accusations that have been made publicly. Nothing but abject honesty and full disclosure will do.

I can support acknowledgement of the deficiency and solid evidence of positive actions to address the issue through amends to the body and training of staff and volunteers on the proper way to handle threats to those in the body.

If mismanagement and poor leadership comes out in the truth of these events, I can support dismissal or remedial actions taken against the individual(s) involved.

I have no desire to create a rift, nor do I have an agenda. I just want answers to my questions in a public setting where others can hear my questions and also hear your answers.

As a co-dependent personality who struggles with the effects of abusive relationships, I get the tendency to cope with negative news with silence, hoping the issue will go away. My personal experience shows me that trying to avoid pain by not removing the splinter only leads to festering and infection.

That is where FCCF is today.

It is leadership's role to clean out the infection through open, honest communication with the body of church members that will allow healing to begin. I look forward to participating in a full disclosure meeting of the body, at which your side of the story is told and your positive action plan for the future is revealed.

In His mighty hand, _____.

The Purpose 6

As I have interviewed people associated with this case study, they have asked me, "Why are you writing this story?"

I am not writing this story as one of the elders at the church; I am not writing this story as a law enforcement officer; I am not writing this story as a lawyer; I am not even writing this story as a reporter!

The Victims

I am writing this story for the two victims and any future victims.

These two victims needed protection, but they may feel the church failed them. They need a voice now, but they may feel they are being ignored. They will need patient and loving support and care—but they may believe the church will not provide it.

Their families, likewise, will need patient and loving support and care as they work through this with their children.

Other victims exist. Titus and I have communicated with another alleged victim, and we have been told of allegations of other possible alleged victims from FCCF—in addition to these two. The other alleged victims are terrified to come forward—they dislike themselves; they distrust the church; they disbelieve in God.

I empathize with the victims. At 10, I was a victim of abuse, multiple times, by a middle-aged married man, a neighbor across the street. At 18, I was a victim of a sexual assault by a college student, a well-known senior from my dorm. I did not report either incident. I regret not doing so. I kept silent for over 20 years — I will not keep silent now.

One former youth minster hoped that this document would "open communication and allow other victims a chance to heal, and the current victims a chance to feel loved by the church they trusted."[200]

I pray this story would help these two victims and their families; I pray this story would help any other victims to come forward — sooner than later — and experience the true restoration and forgiveness found only in Christ.

The Church

I am writing this story for the youth ministers, sponsors, parents, kids, staff, teachers, church members.

They are all victims, collateral victims, for they were betrayed, deceived, and fooled by Brandon's actions.

Many live with a deep-seated anger over the broken trust but may also live with a deep sadness to see such a talented and gifted young minister — with a productive future — spend that future in prison. The church needs to process this story; lessons are waiting to be learned. Titus recently blogged about three things the church must learn: The church must get better at recognizing, preventing, and dealing with sexual abuse.[201] Powerful advice. I would add a fourth. The church must get better at pastoring the casualties of sexual abuse — the primary victims and the many collateral victims.

I pray this story would bring to light the darkness of sexual abuse, so we, the church, can bring to the victims, the families, and the church the light of the gospel of restoration.

---

[200] Facebook message received on March 17, 2015.

[201] Titus Benton, "What I've Learned Since My Friend Got Arrested," Titus Live, February 12, 2015, http://tituslive.com/2015/02/12/what-ive-learned-since-my-friend-got-arrested/.

The Elders

I am writing this story for the senior minister and the elders of FCCF, the overseers of the church.

As a former elder and pastor, I understand the role they play in the church. If I were an elder or staff member at FCCF, I would want to know about any and all allegations of sexual abuse. A youth sponsor did come forward three years ago.

The elders are the protectors of the church's most vulnerable treasure—our kids. The elders need to take responsibility for their handling of the situation—investigate all of the alleged allegations, examine the procedures and policies of the church, and take swift and corrective measures with any personnel found to be culpable. The elders cannot continue to be silent.

The college where I was assaulted was silent. Although they had received numerous allegations and complaints about the student who had sexually assaulted me, the college allowed—by their silence—this student to enter into full-time campus ministry and remain there for nearly 20 years. He worked among the very young people from whom he would solicit sex.

The FCCF leadership was informed about serious alleged allegations against Brandon two years before his arrest, yet he was allowed—by their silence—to continue to minister to the very same type of kids from whom he had abused five years earlier.

The elders were mailed a copy of the first edition of this story on March 3, 2015—the five elders, the executive minister[202] and the senior minister.[203] They were mailed a second document with additional information on March 6, 2015. They were mailed a document (Why I am Writing....) on March 9, 2015. On March 15, 2015, the elders were mailed a fourth document, a compilation of these three documents, and on March 23, 2015, the elders were sent this fifth edition—including the response of the elders. As the spiritual shepherds of FCCF, they were the first ones to read this story; they will not be, however, the last ones.

---

[202] He was hired in February 2015 as the executive minister and ordained on March 15, 2015. Previously, he was the chairman of the elders.

[203] He is also an elder.

I pray this story would move the elders to "shepherd the flock . . . not domineering over those in their charge, but as examples to the flock."[204]

The Predators

I am writing this story for predators to warn them that the church is on high alert to the signs of a sexual predator.

The constant thread throughout this story has been that people saw "nothing obvious." Brandon hid in plain sight. He fooled others; he fooled us; he fooled me.

Predators, like Brandon, are masters of deception — by building coalitions with those in authority to help them hide their behavior. If suspicions are suspected, they rally around their supporters to fight for them, as was the case at FCCF with the senior minister and the executive minister. If confronted with allegations of abuse, they deny them with a calm and reassuring demeanor, as was the case when I confronted Brandon about the alleged allegations of 2012. If they are confronted with suspicions, they quickly apologize, as was the case when Brandon was caught with a middle-school kid in his dorm room. They divert the attention off of themselves.

I pray this story would help to instruct not only churches and colleges but also the population at large by identifying the "signs" of abuse before the abuse happens — to help stop the predators before they start.

Brandon Milburn

I am writing this story for Brandon Milburn, guilty of seven counts of sodomy of two minors under the age of 12.

I first met Brandon when he came in and sat in my office at the college; he was an incoming freshman, and I was his academic advisor. And now, nearly 10 years later, he sits in a jail cell in St. Louis County; he is now a convicted sex offender, and I am his former advisor, professor, and mentor, wrestling with the events of the past ten years. Predators need justice; his justice will come in a few weeks as he awaits a sentence between 10 years to life.

---

[204] 1 Peter 5:3.

But predators also need the gospel. During several visits with Brandon in jail this past year, I have wondered how he will adapt to life in prison. How will justice and mercy be carried out in his life? Will he repent? Will he seek forgiveness from the victims? Will he seek reconciliation with the church? Will he allow the Lord to turn this tragedy into something good?

I pray this story would help Brandon, and other predators behind bars, to receive and experience the gospel of Christ — the gospel of forgiveness and reconciliation.

Is It Enough? 7

Is it enough to deny the existence of other alleged victims? Is it enough to ignore the pain of the collateral victims? Is it enough to keep silent about the church's responsibility towards dealing with sexual abuse? Is it enough to remain ignorant to the signs of sexual predators? Is it enough to miss the opportunity to learn from the mistakes of this tragedy — thus turning evil into good?

It is not enough for me to close the book on this story — I will continue to turn on the light and turn the pages of this story. Should it not be enough for you too?[205]

Sentencing 8

Justice took nearly 8 years. The sexual abuse began on June 1, 2007, and the sentencing ended on March 30, 2015, at around 12:45 p.m., 25 years for seven counts of sodomy.

---

[205] It is with the upmost care and prayer that we have researched the dates and places mentioned in this case study, interviewed individuals related to its content, and written with clarity and truthfulness, as we understand the events. We have not knowingly or willfully falsified or altered the facts to deceive or defame any individuals. We still continue to investigate, rework, revise, and update the information in this story. If anyone knows of any inaccuracies with the dates, places, or events, or knows of any necessary information that is absent or omitted, please contact Douglas Lay at **isitenough15@gmail.com.** We will investigate all responses, and if any corrections, alterations, or admissions are found to be accurate, we will include the information in the revised edition. As of this writing, the senior minister and all additional full-time staff members at FCCF, along with all five elders. have yet to comment on, edit, alter, add, or deny any information presented herein. Attempts continue to be made to add their perspectives to this case study. The objective of this case study is to collect, analyze, and assimilate any and all information pertaining to this story.

Contributors

Douglas Lay

I am a professor of English and TESOL at Saint Louis Christian College since 1999, a pastor in Fenton, MO, and a missionary in Puerto Rico for nearly 14 years, having taught English for five years at the University of Puerto Rico in Mayaguez.

I was one of Brandon's professors at SLCC and his only academic advisor from August 2005 until May 2011. I was also his mentor, spending time with him outside of the classroom, eating lunch together, and sharing life.

I am a member of First Christian Church of Florissant since 1999. I have taught high school Sunday school classes, volunteered at VBS, co-taught a college-age Sunday school class with Titus, co-taught the college-age Sunday school class with Joe Mueller, occasionally speak on Wednesday evenings, and currently co-teach an adult Sunday school class with my wife, a class previously taught by a former staff member, Steve Ross. I participated in a mission trip to Joplin after the tornado, and, for a short time, was a member of the choir. I am also a survivor of sexual abuse and sexual assault.

Titus Benton

I served at First Christian Church of Florissant first in part-time roles while a student at Saint Louis Christian College ('01 – '03), as full-time intern in '03 – '04, and in a full-time pastoral role from Fall 2005 to June 2011. While there I served alongside Brandon Milburn in our student ministry. Brandon was someone I gave a ton of responsibility to. We worked closely together in a variety of ways.

I never suspected any misconduct on his part, and no one ever approached me with allegations against him during my time on staff. Since learning that his crimes are not limited to the charges brought against him, I have done my best to create an atmosphere where additional victims would feel safe coming forward, including cooperating with the formation and sharing of this document.